MADEIRA
A BOTANICAL
MELTING POT

OLIVER BREDA EDITION

O L I V E R   B R E D A   E D I T I O N

Susanne Lipps

Madeira
A Botanical Melting Pot!

OLIVER BREDA EDITION

THE AUTHOR

Dr. Susanne Lipps is successful author of a number of travel and walking guides about Madeira, the Canary Islands, Spain and Portugal. After having studied Geography, Geology and Botany in Marburg (Germany), she graduated in 1985. Since 1988 she works as tour guide and freelance author and travels regularly to the island of Madeira.

All items in this book have been carefully enquired and checked to the best of our knowledge. The use of this book is at one's owne risk. Author and publisher will not assume any liability for possible damages or prejudices of any kind.

Layout: Günther Roeder, Oliver Breda
Photographs: Susanne Lipps, Oliver Breda
Production: Druckhaus Cramer, Greven
Translation: Daniela Overkamp

© Oliver Breda Verlag, Duisburg
E-mail: webmaster@bredaverlag.de
1. Edition 2006

ISBN 3-938282-09-6

CONTENT

Introduction

Madeira definitely deserves its cognomen "Flower Island". In a very confined space there are growing plants from all regions of the earth. Wherever you go numerous plants, both known and unknown will surround you. The botanical guide "Madeira- A Botanical Melting Pot!" is directed to everyone who visits the island and is interested in its flora. The format of the book was chosen to make it possible for everybody to carry it with him/her without being bothered.

Arriving on Madeira you will probably experience the sumptuous flora for the first time in the hotel garden. In the following days you can visit the numerous parks that are all well worth seeing. Colourful plants, most of them native to the tropics, thrive in all of them.

Definitely worth visiting regions with particular vegetation are to be found along the coast. You will find a more inconspicuous but nevertheless interesting flora. Outside the towns the indigenous flora is often well preserved and mixed with numerous foreign species from distant lands.

Eye-catching hotchpotches of different plants are to be found along the famous irrigation channels (levadas) and tiny terrace fields. Strollers and hikers will encounter exotic tropical and subtropical plants next to familiar ones that also grow in British and Central European gardens

In contrast to the vegetation form described earlier, the laurel forest has remained a nearly unspoiled jungle. Apart from the various members of the Laurel family you will encounter numerous trees, shrubs and herbs that have adapted to the humid conditions. Ferns, mosses and lichens give this biotope its somehow primeval appearance. Hikers find a network of paths in the laurel forest.

Rocks characterize the bleak landscape in the centre of the island where you will find heath forests and moors. A sparse, alpine flora populates both steep rocks around the highest mountain peaks and rocky sites at lower altitudes. Finally we should not forget the useful plants that are cultivated on Madeira. Many tropical fruits are grown and sold on the markets. Bananas and sugar cane are of special importance. Apparently familiar plants present themselves in different forms on Madeira.

All in all you will experience the abundance of most different plants on Madeira yourself when you visit the island. The plants that are described in this book can thus only be a selection, completeness can not be claimed. Anyway there are indicated most of the plants that you will encounter during your holiday on Madeira. We wish you a pleasant stay! Susanne Lipps and Oliver Breda

Hints for the usage of this book

The botanical guide **"Madeira- A Botanical Melting Pot!"** contains plant descriptions that are organized in six typical groups. The chosen order corresponds to the order in which the visitor will probably encounter the respective flora: exotic plants introduced from tropical and subtropical countries in gardens and parks, wild growing vegetation in coastal areas, flora of cultivated land and along irrigation channels (levadas), vegetation of the laurisilva / laurel forest, flora in the mountains and on rock faces, typical useful plants.

There may be plants that cannot be clearly assigned to one of the chapters. They will be described with the vegetation form that is their most typical habitat. In order to not oversize the book you will not find descriptions neither of plants that were introduced to Madeira from Europe (maples, oaks, firs) nor of ornamental plants that are commonly known (geranium, narcissus, etc.)

Within the different chapters the plants are organized from big to small. The details about the **bloom time** are guidelines. The climate on Madeira is very uniform; thus it is possible that several specimens of various species bloom at all times of the year (especially in years with an unusual weather development). You should be able to clearly identify the plants on the basis of the images and the pieces of information that are given about their **characteristics**, even if you don't have any special botanical knowledge. The **site** details offer information about sites where you can easily encounter the respective plants. The plant descriptions are completed with **interesting pieces of information** that are directly or indirectly linked with the plant in question.

The last chapter is dedicated to Madeira's most beautiful **parks**. There you find information about the history of each garden, a detailed description and supplementary facts about opening hours, prices and how to get there by bus or by rented car. You will need a **map** of the island to find the parks and the sites that are indicated within the plant descriptions. Tour operators and hotels hand out general maps and a map of Funchal to their guests. It is also available free of charge in the tourist offices and will do for gaining a first overview. The Walking map of Madeira 1:50000 by Goldstadt is more detailed and also suited as a road map. It is available in many Madeiran bookstores.

The detailed **register** lists the botanical denomination and the common English names of the plants. In public parks and gardens, many plants are labelled with the botanical denomination; thus it will not be difficult to find already identified plants in the book.

In the Gardens

Madeira's cognomen "Flower Island" is due to the tropical and subtropical flora that thrives in the gardens and parks and decorates avenues, roadsides and promenades. The cultivated plants were imported from all over the world and impress either with their outstanding flowers or with their conspicuous shape. The less spectacular endemic flora is only scarcely represented in the gardens. Exceptions prove the rule (e. g. the decorative dragon tree, the sumptuous endemic viper's buglosses, Canary marguerites and Madeira stork's bills). In the 16th century, Portuguese seafarers began to introduce plants from Africa, Asia and South America to Madeira that had been unknown in Europe until then. They intended to adapt the delicate, tropical species gradually to a chillier climate so that later they would be able to cultivate them outside in Portugal, e.g. in the royal gardens of Lisbon and Sintra. This aim was never achieved because many tropical plants do not tolerate temperatures of only several degrees above zero or lower. Anyway, Madeira's flora was enriched. In the 18th and 19th century British wine merchants mostly impressed the island, both economically and culturally. They also imported numerous exotic plants. They used to construct villas at more dizzy altitudes of 500-700 m (550-765 yd.) where the climate is less sultry than in the coastal areas and vied with each other to collect botanical rarities from all continents. They introduced mostly subtropical plants from South Africa, Australia, New Zealand and Japan to Madeira and sometimes from there to England. Many trees and shrubs originate in the more moderate climate zones of North America and thrive in gardens at higher altitudes.

Today both public authorities and private people continue the traditional garden culture. Every roadside and every traffic island is carefully planted with Oleander, Sword Aloe, Agapanthus and Hydrangea. All plants flower at different times of the year. Thus the visitor always feels like being "on a swimming garden in the middle of the Atlantic". Every garden, whether big or small, is well tended by its owner. The most beautiful plantings are valued with prices and honours in all villages. Many ornamental plants that are also known in Central and West Europe nowadays, are decorating kitchen gardens (e.g. fuchsias, freesias, geraniums and petunias). A multitude of gardeners is continually working for the care and the (re)planting of plants in the big parks that are open to the public. Mostly at these sites people fond of botany will find magnificent trees, shrubs and flowering plants from tropical and subtropical countries.

Australian Tree Fern, Cooper's Tree Fern
Sphaeropteris cooperi

Bloom time
None

Characteristics

The giant fern produces a thin trunk that grows up to 9 m (10 yd.) tall and thus reminds of a palm tree. The fronds branch from the top of the trunk; they are remarkably longer than 1 m (3,3') and bipinnate. You will easily observe scars on the trunk's bark; they derive from elder fronds that have already fallen off.

Site:
Cooper's Tree Fern is cultivated in moist regions up to an altitude of 800 m (875 yd.). It is frequently found in shady ravines as in the "Inferno" in Palheiro Gardens. Some remarkable specimens can also be found in the region of Ribeiro Frio, along the Levada da Serra superior to Camacha and on the central square of Camacha.

Interesting to know:
Cooper's Tree Fern is native to Australia. Nowadays it has spread worldwide through tropical and subtropical regions because of its highly decorating character. Although you only find slight variations there are known about 900 species of tree ferns. They grow in mountain forests mainly on the southern hemisphere. To grow well they require a stable climate with a constantly high humidity and without frost. The trunks do no consist of wood; they are tubes that are supported by the surrounding stalks and aerial roots.

KING SAGO PALM
CYCAS REVOLUTA

BLOOM TIME
All year round.

CHARACTERISTICS

The King Sago Palm looks like a crossbreed between a fern and a palm but only grows up to 3 m (10') tall. The trunk is sturdy and scaly. The fronds reach a length of about 2 m (6,6'). In the centre of the crown are growing the plant's brown blooms: female specimens develop a woolly hemisphere, males a cone.

SITE:
On Madeira you will find the King Sago Palm in various gardens, mainly in regions at an altitude of 300-600 m (330-655 yd.). An impressing collection of Cycas, including a variety of other species than the King Sago Palm, is to be found in the Jardim Tropical Monte Palace.

INTERESTING TO KNOW:
Cycas are very old representatives of flowering plants. They already existed in the days of the dinosaurs, approx. 200 million years ago and thus are frequently referred to as "living fossils". Today the majority of the 185 known species is threatened with extinction. The King Sago Palm, native to South-East Asia, is especially resistant and can even be grown in Mediterranean regions. Younger specimens are popular as houseplants. All Cycas are toxic. The seed of the King Sago Palm only becomes edible by roasting or drying it.

NORFOLK ISLAND PINE (MIDDLE-LEFT)
ARAUCARIA EXCELSA

BLOOM TIME
March and April.

CHARACTERISTICS

The Norfolk Island Pine is a giant conifer that can reach a height superior to 50 m (55 yd.). At each level, six branches emerge nearly horizontally from the trunk. The quite long distance between the various branch levels produces the picture of a relatively sparse crown.

SITE:
The Norfolk Island Pine grows in many parks up to an altitude of 600 m (655 yd.); as a decorative specimen tree it often towers above all other plants. It is frequently cultivated next to the Bunya Pine (Araucaria bidwillii); this tree reaches a similar height but is characterized by a rounded off crown (right side of the picture).

INTERESTING TO KNOW:
Initially the genus Araucaria was restricted to the southern hemisphere. Two of its species are native to South America; the remaining 16 species are native to Australia and the South-West Pacific. The Norfolk Island Pine's natural habitat is Norfolk Island (Pacific Ocean, east of Australia). Today it is cultivated as an ornamental plant in parks in regions with a warm and humid climate. The high demand of wooden masts in times of giant sailing ships helped this species with its very straight growing trunk to spread worldwide.

BLUE LAWSON'S CYPRESS
CHAMAECYPARIS LAWSONIANA

BLOOM TIME
April and May.

CHARACTERISTICS
3-10 m (3-11 yd.) high, the light green conifer is known for growing evenly and conically. Younger specimens develop their needles right above the ground; elder specimens develop a short trunk. The inflorescences are inconspicuous and barely to be noticed. The spherical cones are slightly blue.

SITE:
The Blue Lawson's Cypress flourishes in all regions at 600-1300 m (655-1420 yd.) altitude that are the natural habitat of the laurel forest. You will find various specimens both in the parks (e.g. Quinta do Santo da Serra) and along the roadside. Moreover it grows in exotic collections of trees that have been cultivated in projects by forest management services (e.g. lining the road from the Poiso pass to Ribeiro Frio).

INTERESTING TO KNOW:
This attractive conifer is native to North America, mainly to the northwest of the USA. There it grows in big populations and reaches a height up to 50 m (55 yd.). The conical or columnar species of these "false" cypresses are cultivated as ornamental plants in these regions that are not supported by the similar genuine cypresses. False cypresses are more resistant and grow faster. There have been grown more than 100 horticultural cultivars of Blue Lawson's Cypress.

QUEENSLAND KAURI
AGATHIS BROWNII

BLOOM TIME
March.

CHARACTERISTICS

The tree reaches a height of 10-20 m (11-22 yd.). Its crown is larger in height than in width. The tough leaves are slender and tapered and stick rigidly out from the twigs. The female blooms are light brown, longish and slightly curved cones that are shorter than the leaves. They disintegrate at maturity of the fruits.

SITE:

The Queensland Kauri requires sunlight and warmth, thus you will mainly find it close to the southern coastal line. It barely grows in regions higher than 100 m (110 yd.) above sea level. It is frequently found in the parks and hotel gardens of Funchal and lines roads in the city centre; e.g. the Avenida do Mar or the Avenida do Infante.

INTERESTING TO KNOW:

The tree is native to Northeast Australia. Although seeming to resemble a deciduous tree, Queensland Kauri is a conifer and part of the Araucaria family. The natural habitats of the Araucariaceae can all be found on the southern hemisphere. Two species related to Queensland Kauri, the Borneo Kauri (Agathis dammara), native to the Philippines, and the New Zealand Kauri (Agathis australis), native to New Zealand, are providing wood and kauri resin. The amber-coloured, hard resin is for example used to produce varnishes.

WEEPING FIG
FICUS BENJAMINA

BLOOM TIME
All around the year.

CHARACTERISTICS
The giant tree that may grow up to 20 m (22 yd.) tall can develop various trunks and spreading branches with aerial roots. The oval, tapered leaves are quite small and similar to amber leaves but dispose of a milky sap. The inconspicuous blooms develop fig-like, red fruits (Ø 1 cm (0,4")).

SITE:
You will find the Weeping Fig in parks up to an altitude of 200 m (220 yd.) above sea level. Either as a single tree or in groups it may decorate a square and provide shade simultaneously (e.g. at Largo dos Milagres in Machico, at the viewpoint in Rua das Cruzes, close to the Quinta das Cruzes (Funchal)). It may also line avenues like the Avenida do Mar, Funchal.

INTERESTING TO KNOW:
The Weeping Fig is native to Malaysia; anyway it is cultivated today in many tropical and subtropical countries. Younger specimens are used as indoor trees in many Central European houses. It is closely related to the Indian Rubber Tree (Ficus elastica). The Common Fig Tree (Ficus carica), native to the Mediterranean region, is another representative of this species-rich genus. Single specimens of the latter are cultivated on Madeira as useful plants (mainly in the northeast close to Faial and São Roque do Faial).

15

CAMPHOR TREE, CAMPHOR LAUREL
CINNAMONUM CAMPHORA

BLOOM TIME

From January to April.

CHARACTERISTICS

The tree grows up to 20 m (22 yd.) high and disposes of a very close branch network. Together with its dense foliage this creates a spreading crown. The ovate, tapered leaves turn upwards remarkably feebly. The great number of inconspicuous, greenish blooms branches erectly from thin panicles.

SITE:

The Camphor Tree is one of the most impressing trees that grows in Madeira's parks. It prefers warm, sheltered sites close to the southern coast. You will mainly find it in Funchal, e.g. in the Parque Santa Catarina or in the Quinta Magnólia.

INTERESTING TO KNOW:

The Camphor Tree is indigenous to China, Taiwan and Japan where it is admired for its giant stature and for being able to become hundreds of years old. Today it is recognized as an ornamental tree in all warm countries. The Camphor Tree resembles laurels and is assigned to the same family. Being crumbled, the leaves smell of camphor. Initially, camphor oil was produced by distilling it from the shavings. It has already been employed for centuries both externally against rheumatism and internally to support the heart functions.

BRAZILIAN KAPOK TREE, PINK FLOSS SILK TREE
CEIBA SPECIOSA

BLOOM TIME
September and October

CHARACTERISTICS
The trunk can grow up to 15 m (16 yd.) tall and tapers remarkably in upward direction. It is covered with conical spines. The hand-shaped leaves fall off in spring. The pear-shaped fruits contain a silky substance. The five-petaled, pink flowers develop before the new leaves emerge.

SITE:
In the southern half of Madeira you will frequently find the Brazilian Kapok Tree up to an altitude of 350 m (385 yd.). It lines roads and decorates parks and gardens. Beautiful specimens can be contemplated e.g. in the Jardim Municipal (Funchal) and in the garden of the Quinta Vigia. In Machico you will find a Kapok Tree next to the town hall.

INTERESTING TO KNOW:
The Brazilian Kapok Tree is native to the savannahs of Brazil and Argentina. The fruits contain about 100 black seeds with white, woolly hairs that are distributed by wind. The Common Kapok Tree/Silk Cotton Tree (Ceiba pentandra) that does not grow on Madeira but is cultivated on Asian plantations disposes of seed hairs that are of commercial value. They are waxy and do not absorb water - thus they are used to produce life jackets, lifebelts and mattresses.

17

Sausage Tree, Fetish Tree
Kigelia africana

Bloom time
From June to August.

Characteristics

The colour of the trumpet-shaped blossoms ranges from deep red to purple. They hang in loose panicles on long stalks. The typical sausage-like fruits are developing from the blossoms. Some are longish, others bulbous. The leaves of this tree that reaches a height of 5 m (5,5 yd.) are pinnate and fall off in winter.

Site:
You will find the Sausage Tree growing only in the south up to an altitude of 100 m (110 yd.). It is hardly ever cultivated in gardens and parks. Three beautiful specimens are situated in the Jardim Municipal in Funchal, another one in the Parque Santa Catarina. Two other specimens are to be found in the Quinta Magnólia.

Interesting to know:
The Sausage Tree is indigenous to West Africa. In this humid and warm regions it grows up to 20 m (22 yd.); the fruits may be up to 1 m (3,3') long and weigh up to 10 kg. The specimens that grow in Madeira's gardens do not reach these dimensions. The fleshy fruits are inedible; anyway they are used in Africa by traditional medicine and magic. They are supposed to cure rheumatism, snake bits and syphilis as well as to protect from evil ghosts. The flowers only blossom one night. At daytime you only see buds or wilted blooms.

AFRICAN TULIP TREE,
FLAME OF THE FOREST
SPATHODEA CAMPANULATA

BLOOM TIME
All year round.

CHARACTERISTICS
The decorative tree can reach a height up to 25 m (28 yd.). Its dark green leaves are pinnate. Round inflorescences are situated on the surface of the dense, spherical crown. The tulip-like flowers are coloured from orange to scarlet and are slightly curved towards the centre of the blossom cluster.

SITE:
In the southern coastal area of Madeira you will frequently find the tree as an ornamental plant up to an altitude of 200 m (220 yd.). It lines town roads and grows in gardens and parks. In Funchal you find some specimens in the Parque Santa Catarina, in the Avenida do Infante and in the Avenida Luis Camões that leads towards the hospital.

INTERESTING TO KNOW:
The tree is native to the African savannahs where, in contrast to Madeira, it sheds its leaves in the arid season. Today it is one of the most popular ornamental plants in all countries that correspond to its climatic requirements. It is a fast growing tree; the wood is hardly usable. The outer buds bloom first while the inner, brown and hairy buds still remain closed. Birds in search of nectar will land on the latter ones. On Madeira, pollination is not taking place.

In the Gardens

Blue Jacaranda,
Brazilian Rosewood
Jacaranda mimosifolia

Bloom time
From April to May.

Characteristics
The gnarled growing tree grows up to 20 m (22 yd.) tall. In winter it sheds off its leaves. Before they sprout again in spring the bleak tree develops the popular blue-violet panicles of flowers. They consist of many single blossoms. As those of many fern species, the tender leaves are bipinnate.

Site:
In the south of Madeira the Blue Jacaranda is growing in gardens and parks up to an altitude of 300 m (330 yd.). In Funchal, Jacaranda is lining whole streets. There you may discover an especially conspicuous effect of the flowers at the end of April when they produce strongly violet shining avenues, e.g. in Avenida Arriaga, in Avenida do Infante or in Rua João de Deus.

Interesting to know:
The tree origins from the savannahs of South Brazil. The Portuguese explorers adapted the Indian name: the "j" at the beginning is pronounced like in journal, the emphasis is on the last syllable. Today Jacaranda is cultivated in many countries because of its spectacular flowers. It is said that in Pretoria (South Africa) there are cultivated 6000 specimens.

PRIDE OF BOLIVIA, TIPU TREE
TIPUANA TIPU

BLOOM TIME

From June to September; during this time there are constantly emerging new blossoms.

CHARACTERISTICS

The imposing tree has dense foliage and a broad crown. It grows up to 10 m (11 yd.) tall. The long leaves are pinnate; the single compounds are longish and ovate. The yellow blossoms emerge from short panicles.

SITE:

Although you may find the Pride of Bolivia on Madeira in regions up to an altitude of 600 m (655 yd.), it mainly grows in coastal areas. Especially in Funchal the tree is lining many roads, e.g. the Avenida Zarco or the Rua Arcipreste behind the market hall.

INTERESTING TO KNOW:

The tree is native to South America (Brazil, Argentina, Bolivia) where it can grow up to 35 m (38 yd.) tall. Its botanical denomination refers to the Valle Tipuana, a Bolivian valley in which the Tipu Tree develops larger populations. It belongs to the family of Fabaceae; thus it is not related to Jacaranda (Bignonia family, cf. p. 20). Anyway it is also called Yellow Jacaranda because of its pinnate leaves and blossom panicles. Pride of Bolivia is a fast growing, undemanding and flexible tree, characteristics that make it popular as a street tree. Today it is even cultivated in mild regions of the Mediterranean.

FLAME TREE
BRACHYCHITON ACERIFOLIUM

BLOOM TIME

From April to September.

CHARACTERISTICS

The Flame Tree grows up to 10 m (11 yd.) tall. The leaves consist of three to five lobes and are shed off in winter. In spring the plant develops the main blossoms before new leaves sprout. The scarlet blossoms are little and bell-shaped; they grow in long, hanging racemes.

SITE:

At Madeira's southern coast you will often find the Flame tree being cultivated as an ornamental plant up to an altitude of 200 m (220 yd.). You may frequently see the plant in Funchal where it is both lining roads and growing in gardens and parks. An eye-catching specimen shades the inner courtyard of Funchal's market hall.

INTERESTING TO KNOW:

The tree is native to Australia where it grows in the rainforest at the eastern coast. In South Africa you might see it frequently as a park tree. Its frost tolerance allows cultivating it even in the Mediterranean regions. The wood is extremely light and soft; thus you could hammer against the trunks of older specimens and will notice that they sound empty. The wood is sometimes employed to produce life belts; moreover it can serve as a substitute for balsa wood in model construction.

TROPICAL HYDRANGEA TREE,
PINK BALL DOMBEYA
DOMBEYA WALLICHII

BLOOM TIME
From November to February.

CHARACTERISTICS

The tree grows spherically and reaches up to 8 m (9 yd.) tall. It has dense foliage. The heart-shaped leaves are tapered, have a pointed extreme and are tenderly hairy on the underside. The hemispherical, hanging flowers remind of Hydrangeas. The single blossoms are pink with yellow stamens.

SITE:
You will find the Hydrangea Tree in parks in the south, mainly in the region of Funchal and up to an altitude of 300 m (330 yd.). Specimen trees are growing in the Botanical Garden, in the Quinta das Cruzes and in the Quinta Palmeira.

INTERESTING TO KNOW:
The tree is native to Madagascar. Today it is cultivated as an ornamental plant in all tropical countries. Despite of its name and the blossoms it is not related to Hydrangeas but belongs to the Mallow family (Malvaceae). The genus Dombeya got its name from J. Dombey (1742-1795), popular as a traveller for America, and contains about 300 species that are exclusively native to Africa, mainly to Madagascar. Their blossoms are not too attractive yet. Anyway some Dombeya species from South Africa are cultivated in the Mediterranean region because they tolerate light frosts (in contrast to the Tropical Hydrangea Tree).

Batwing Coral Tree
Erythrina speciosa

Bloom time
From January to April.

Characteristics
The tree grows up to 5 m (5,5 yd.) tall. The heart-shaped leaves are shed off in winter. Blossoms sprout of the bare tree. The conical inflorescences are placed at the shoot tips; mostly in little groups on short sprigs. The intense red single blooms have crescent-like ends that rigidly stick out sideways.

Site:
On Madeira you will find the Batwing Coral Tree as an ornamental plant in parks and gardens. It prefers sites in the sunny southern part of the island up to an altitude of 300 m (330 yd.). For example there are several specimens situated in the Parque Santa Catarina, Funchal. You can also find the tree growing in Machico and in Ribeira Brava.

Interesting to know:
The Batwing Coral Tree is native to South Brazil. The Abyssinian Coral Tree/Red-Hot Poker Tree (Erythrina abyssinica) is a related species indigenous to Central and East Africa with brush-shaped flowers. The lobes of the single blossom are narrower and thread-shaped. This species can also be found on Madeira. The seeds of most Coral Tree species are toxic. The seeds of Abyssinian Coral Tree contain a narcotic agent that has a similar effect to curare. It could cause paralysis or even death for human beings.

COCK'S COMB CORAL TREE
ERYTHRINA CRISTA-GALLI

BLOOM TIME
From March to September.

CHARACTERISTICS

It can grow up to 5 m (6,5 yd.) tall but often stays shrub-shaped. The leathery leaves are roughly pinnate and partly thorny. You can easily distinguish between the Cock's Comb Coral Tree and other Coral Tree species represented on Madeira by its blossoms that resemble the comb of a rooster.

SITE:
In the south of the island you will find specimen trees in parks and gardens up to an altitude of 300 m (330 yd.). A remarkably giant specimen grows in front of the church on the main square of Caniço. Occasionally you may also encounter this attractive plant in Funchal.

INTERESTING TO KNOW:
The tree originates from tropical regions in South America (South Brazil, Paraguay, Uruguay, North Argentina) where it is pollinated by hummingbirds that are drawn by the conspicuous red blossoms. To attract birds the plant produces particularly much nectar that often drips from the blossoms. Thus the tree is also called "Cry-Baby". The plant tolerates low frost. Although it uses to freeze back there, it can even be cultivated outdoors in Southern England. Being quite hardy and undemanding you may often find it being cultivated in unheated greenhouses of botanical gardens.

JUDAS TREE
CERCIS SILIQUASTRUM

BLOOM TIME
From March to May.

CHARACTERISTICS
The little tree grows up to 5 m (5,5 yd.) tall and sheds off its rounded leaves in winter. The magenta blossoms remind of those of papilionaceous plants. They appear before the leaves emerge and are situated in short racemes directly on the twigs (stem-flowering or cauliflory), often lining them entirely.

SITE:
On Madeira you will probably not find the Judas Tree very frequently. It prefers quite chilly and foggy sites at an altitude of 300-600 m (330-655 yd.) where it grows in several parks, e.g. in the Palheiro Gardens.

INTERESTING TO KNOW:
The tree is native to the bush lands of the eastern Mediterranean regions and the Near East. Its name is derived from "Judaea tree", denomination that refers to its geographical origin. The legend tells us that Judas Iscariot hung himself on a tree of this species after realizing the consequences he had caused by betraying Christ. The plant's blossoms are supposed to symbolize his blood. Its flat seeds are representing the coins that Judas received by the authorities as the reward for his treason.

CAPE CHESTNUT TREE
CALODENDRUM CAPENSE

BLOOM TIME
From May to July.

CHARACTERISTICS

The tree reaches a height of 7-15 m (7,5-16,5 yd.) and has a smooth trunk with many branches and a broad canopy. The leaves are up to 20 cm (8") long and remind of Sweet Chestnut Trees but appear separately. The conical inflorescences are pink and consist of numerous blooms which each have five narrow petals.

SITE:
The Cape Chestnut Tree does not appear very frequently on Madeira. Occasionally you may find it in several parks and gardens, mostly in the municipal area of Funchal or for example in the Palheiro Gardens.

INTERESTING TO KNOW:
The Cape Chestnut Tree originates from regions that are close to the South African coast. It was introduced as an ornamental plant in many tropical and subtropical countries for its attractive blossoms. The plant is a member of the Rue family (Rutaceae) and thus is not closely related to the Sweet Chestnut Tree, which belongs to the Beech family (Fagaceae). Horse Chestnut Trees make up another family. Rutaceae are nearly exclusively found in warmer zones of the earth. Both leaves and fruits contain ethereal oils. Oranges and lemons are popular representatives of the Rue family.

Peruvian Pepper Tree
Schinus molle

BLOOM TIME

From October to February; fruit bearing from May onwards..

CHARACTERISTICS

The tree grows up to 8 m (9 yd.) tall. With its pendulous twigs it reminds of a Weeping Willow. If you crumble the pinnate, likewise pendulous leaves they smell intensively of pepper. Green berries that become pink at maturity develop from the whitish, inconspicuous flowers organized in panicles.

SITE:

On Madeira you will mainly find Peruvian Pepper Trees as ornamental plants at the southern coast, up to an altitude of 400 m (440 yd.). They are most frequently cultivated in the parks and gardens of Funchal; e.g. there are various specimens to be found in the Parque Santa Catarina.

INTERESTING TO KNOW:

The Peruvian Pepper Tree is not only native to Peru - as implies the denomination - but to all tropical sites in Latin America from Argentina to Mexico. It is not related to the Black Pepper Plant (Piper nigrum), which provides authentic pepper. The fruits also taste hot but somewhat bitter and resinous; in former times they were used to thin down the expensive authentic pepper. The "pink berries" that are on the market today use to be fruits from the Brazilian Pepper Tree (Schinus terebinthifolius). They are toxic in larger quantities and should thus be used thriftily.

TRICOLOURED FRANGIPANI, TRICOLOURED TEMPLE TREE
PLUMERIA TRICOLOR

BLOOM TIME

From June to October; single blossoms all year round.

CHARACTERISTICS

The tree grows up to 6 m (6,5 yd.) tall; first branches emerge shortly above the ground. The gnarled branches contain a milky sap and form a broad crown. The dark green leaves are large and longish. They are shed up during blooming time and leave scars. The flowers are coloured cream-pink or cream-orange.

SITE:

The Tricoloured Frangipani grows in parks and gardens in south coast areas up to an altitude of 300 m (330 yd.). In Funchal, beautiful specimens are to be found in the Parque Santa Catarina and in the Jardim Municipal.

INTERESTING TO KNOW:

The Tricoloured Frangipani is indigenous to Mexico and the northern part of South America. The wild form has white blossoms with a yellow base. Today the cultivars are mostly grown in tropical Asia. As a symbol of eternal life they are commonly planted in temple areas and on graveyards together with the Singapore Frangipani (Plumeria obtusa). Frangipani was the name of the Italian producer of a popular perfume in the 12th century. It is said that when Europeans discovered the tree centuries later in America, the strong fragrance of the blossoms reminded them of this perfume. On Madeira you can also find the Red Frangipani.

Purple Orchid Tree, Camel's Foot Tree
Bauhinia variegata

Bloom time
From January to April.

Characteristics

On Madeira the tree will not grow more than 4 m (4,5 yd.) tall. It has long, thick twigs and silver leaves that hang on short stalks. They are clearly notched at the tip and give the impression of two leaves having grown into one another. The single blossoms are 10 cm (4") broad and coloured pink or narrow purple.

Site:
The Purple Orchid Tree is a rare ornamental plant in the gardens and parks of the south. Next to the entrance to the carport of the casino of Funchal you will find a beautiful specimen. Others are to be seen in the Parque Santa Catarina and in the Botanical Garden.

Interesting to know:
The tree is native to regions from India to South China, mostly to the inclinations of the Himalayas. Today it is cultivated in many tropical and subtropical countries. Many of the other 300 Bauhinia species are also growing in various gardens worldwide. They are called orchid trees because of their blossoms. One of each five-crown petals is lip-like enlarged; thus they remind of the orchids belonging to the genus Cattleya. Anyway the orchid trees are not related to the orchids. The botanical name is derived from the researchers Johann and Caspar Bauhin (1541-1613 and 1560-1624).

Yellow Angel's Trumpet, White Angel's Trumpet Brugmansia candida

BLOOM TIME
All year round.

CHARACTERISTICS
The up to 4 m (4,4 yd.) tall shrub has numerous, trumpet-like blooms that are up to 20 cm (8") long. The five petals grow together and form the trumpet's "neck". At the verge of the broad opening they run into pointed ends. Young leaves are covered with hairs and slightly serrated, later they become smooth and entire.

SITE:
On Madeira you find Angel's Trumpets in many gardens and parks. They grow in coastal areas and in the south of the Island even up to an altitude of 500 m (550 yd.). Beautiful specimens you will find in the park of the Quinta Vigia, Funchal, and in the Palheiro Gardens.

INTERESTING TO KNOW:
In former days the plants of the genus Brugmansia were assigned to the genus Datura (thorn apple). Today only herbal plants with spiny fruits are classified as Daturas. The Angel's Trumpet is an hybrid of various South American wild species. You may also encounter the Golden Angel's Trumpet (Brugmansia aurea), a similar plant native to the northern Andes that is as well cultivated on Madeira as a garden plant. All parts of Brugmansia plants contain toxic alkaloids. Golden Angel's Trumpet is said to be especially poisonous. Indian medicine men prepare an intoxicating drink from its leaves and seeds.

In the Gardens

Japanese Camellia
Camellia japonica

Bloom time
From January to March.

Characteristics
The Japanese Camellia can reach up to 3 m (10') tall and ranges between shrubs and trees. The leaves are egg-shaped, dark green, leathery and glossy. The flowers that remind of roses develop from numerous buds; they only barely scent. There are pink, red and white kinds of blossoms.

Site:
The Japanese Camellia grows at all sites that are the natural habitat of the warmth preferring part of the laurel forest. In corresponding regions you will find it in parks and gardens. A Camellia avenue is guiding towards the Palheiro Gardens. Especially beautiful Camellias are also to be found in the park of Queimadas, in Ribeiro Frio and in the Quinta do Santo da Serra.

Interesting to know:
Camellias are native to East Asia and were named in the 18th century by the popular natural scientist Linné. He derived their name from the Moravian abbot Camellius who dedicated himself to natural historic studies on the Philippines. Only in the early 19th century the first Camellias came from China and Japan to Italy. Cultivation was continued in Milan and Florence. The wild form does have simple pink flowers. Today there are cultivars with double flowers and in various colours.

COMMON OLEANDER, ROSE BAY
NERIUM OLEANDER

BLOOM TIME
From May to August.

CHARACTERISTICS
The shrub grows up to 3 m (10') tall. The twigs grow upright; the leaves are long, narrow and leathery. Its numerous blooms are mostly white or pink and resemble little wheels for its five petals that are curved clockwise. You may also find strong red flowering, decorative cultivars that use to be stuffed.

SITE:
The Common Oleander grows mainly in the south up to an altitude of about 400 m (440 yd.). It prefers a dry and sunny climate and is cultivated at roadsides or on traffic islands. Moreover you find it decorating parks and gardens.

INTERESTING TO KNOW:
In its natural habitat, the Mediterranean regions, the Common Oleander grows frequently at courses of rivers that dry out seasonally. Already in the ancient world Common Oleander was recognized as an ornamental plant. Depictions of the shrub are to be found on Cretan murals dating from the 14th century BC and in Pompeii. Cross-breedings with the fragrant Sweet-scented Oleander (Nerium odorum) from India produced intensively smelling species. The Common Oleander plant contains substances that could cause cardiac arrest. In South France the pulverized bark is used as rat poison. Even wood and leaves are poisonous.

CHINESE HIBISCUS, ROSE OF CHINA
HIBISCUS ROSA SINENSIS

BLOOM TIME
All year round.

CHARACTERISTICS

The shrub is 1-3 m (3,3-10') tall and develops a dense net of branches. The leaves are heart-shaped and serrated. The blossoms consist of five petals that form a funnel with up to 10 cm (4") width. Colours range from red and pink trough white to orange and yellow. The pistil protrudes far out of the bloom.

SITE:
On Madeira you will find this shrub in parks and gardens up to an altitude of 400 m (440 yd.). For its dense growth it is often used for cultivating hedges. The hardy Rose of Sharon (Hibiscus syriacus) is a rare relative with smaller, pink flowers and very upright twigs.

INTERESTING TO KNOW:
The Chinese Hibiscus is one of the most popular ornamental shrubs. In its native habitat in South East Asia it has already been cultivated for a long time. Female Asians used to colour their hair and eyebrows with the sap. The wild species has shining red blossoms, cultivars may have flowers in varying colours, stuffed or enlarged blossoms and speckled leaves. The blossoms are extremely short living but the abundant development of buds makes up for the fact that each flower will only last one day.

BRAZILIAN SPIDER FLOWER
TIBOUCHINA URVILLEANA

BLOOM TIME
All year round.

CHARACTERISTICS
The shrub grows up to 3 m (10') tall and has oval, tapered, velvety leaves. Each leave is conspicuously subdivided by several longitudinal veins from which are branching smaller, vertical leaf nerves. The flowers consist of five bluish-purple petals. The stamens are thread-shaped and curved like horns.

SITE:
Mainly situated in the north of the island, the Brazilian Spider Flower can be found in gardens and parks at an altitude of 200-700 m (220-765 yd.). It prefers a more shady and humid habitat. You may for example find various specimens in the Quinta do Santo da Serra.

INTERESTING TO KNOW:
The Brazilian Spider Flower is native to Brazil and the adjoining countries. Today it is a popular ornamental plant in all tropical and subtropical regions for its showy blossoms. The genus' name derives from a denomination in a native Guiana language. It was introduced in literature by the French natural scientist Aublet who visited Guiana in 1762. The genus Tibouchina consists of about 250 species, all of them containing plentiful aluminium. The Indian medicine appreciates the plant for its styptic effects.

In the Gardens

POPCORN BUSH,
PEANUT BUTTER CASSIA
SENNA DIDYMOBOTRYA

BLOOM TIME
All year round, mainly in spring and summer.

CHARACTERISTICS
The decorative shrub grows 1,5-3 m (5-13') tall and has upright twigs at which extremes you find several racemes of golden yellow blossoms at erect stalks. The brown buds open from bottom to top; a part of the bud remains closed for a long time. The large, evergreen leaves are monopinnate.

SITE:
The Popcorn Bush is often cultivated on Madeira; most easily you will find it in the south of the island up to an altitude of 450 m (490 yd.). You may also frequently discover the plant not only in the city of Funchal, but also in Caniço and in Caniço de Baixo.

INTERESTING TO KNOW:
The Popcorn Bush is native to tropical East Africa. It is often mixed up with the Candle Bush. Anyway, the latter has yellow buds; thus the entire inflorescence seems to be made of wax. This plant is not cultivated on Madeira. A noticeable characteristic of the Popcorn Bush is the slightly unpleasant smell that is exuded by the leaves or by buds when crumbling them. This smell reminds of rancid peanut butter or old popcorn.

LOBSTER CLAW, PARROT'S BEAK
CLIANTHUS PUNICEUS

BLOOM TIME
From March to May.

CHARACTERISTICS
The shrub with a height up to 2 m (6,6') is easily mixed up with smaller specimens of the related Cock's Comb Coral Tree (cf. p. 25). Anyway, Lobster Claw's clusters of orange flowers hang downwards. Single blossoms remind of parrots' beaks. The leaves are finely pinnate, the twigs are conspicuously curved.

SITE:
On Madeira, Lobster Claw prefers altitudes of 350-700 m (385-765 yd.); anyway it can also be found at coastal levels. It is quite frequently cultivated in gardens, parks and at roadsides - among others mainly in Funchal and Caniço.

INTERESTING TO KNOW:
Lobster Claw is native to New Zealand. For overgrazing of its habitats it is nearly extinct there and ranges among the most threatened plant species of the world. Fortunately it can easily be cultivated. Especially in England it is very popular as an ornamental plant for its dense inflorescence. It tolerates light frost and can thus be grown outdoors. Moreover it is to be found in greenhouses of botanical gardens or in many private vineyards in Central Europe. As a climbing plant it is popular for being grown in hanging baskets or at trellises. Apart from specimens with orange flowers you can find cultivars in pink and white.

STIFF BOTTLEBRUSH
CALLISTEMON RIGIDUS

BLOOM TIME
From April to June.

CHARACTERISTICS

The evergreen shrub grows 1-2 m (3,3-6,6') tall. Its leathery leaves emerge from the twigs like beaters. They remind of a conifer's needles and scent aromatically when crumbling them. Stamens stick out from every single blossom; thus the shining red flower clusters resemble bottlebrushes.

SITE:
On Madeira the Stiff Bottlebrush grows in coastal areas. In the south it reaches up to an altitude of 450 m (490 yd.). Single specimens are decorating various parks and gardens. Among others you can find it in the Parque Santa Catarina or close to the volcanic cave in São Vicente.

INTERESTING TO KNOW:
The Stiff Bottlebrush is native to Southeast Australia and adapted to frequent bush fires. The leaves contain ethereal oils and catch fire that fast that the oxygen is removed from the flame; the twigs hardly do not suffer any damage. The seeds stay with the plant for several years in cone-like groups. They only open and sprout after having been exposed to fire. As they grow among the ashes of a burnt off vegetation they scarcely have any rivals. The similar Weeping Bottlebrush is also cultivated on Madeira. Its leaves are softer; the twigs hang down like those of a Weeping Willow.

KING PROTEA, CAPE ARTICHOKE FLOWER
PROTEA CYNAROIDES

BLOOM TIME:
From April to June.

CHARACTERISTICS:
The plant grows 1-1,5 m (3,3 – 5') tall. The leathery, spatula-shaped leaves are slightly crinkled and shine silvery. The calyces resemble artichokes or thistles. The outer bracts are coloured from violet to pink, the colour of the inner, tubular blooms ranges from a pale violet through green to silver.

SITE:
In the Palheiro Gardens you will find King Proteas growing in two groups. Further protea species with blooms of different colours can be explored as well. Single specimens are to be found in the garden of the Quinta of Prazeres or close to the Quinta do Furão. At some places close to Camacha at an altitude of 400-700 m (440-765 yd.) or in the region above Calheta, proteas are cultivated for commercial purposes.

INTERESTING TO KNOW:
In the 20th century Mildred Blandy directed Blandy's Garden (currently known as the Palheiro Gardens) for five decades. She introduced Proteas to Madeira. She had raised in South Africa and thus felt a special affection for the flora of her motherland. After already being very fashionable in the 19th century, Proteas were rediscovered as cut flowers in the last years. Having been dried they stay attractive for several months.

LESSER BOUGAINVILLEA
BOUGAINVILLEA GLABRA

BLOOM TIME

All year round, mainly in early summer.

CHARACTERISTICS

The thorny climbing plant grows up to 25 m (28 yd.) tall on (building) walls. The leaves don't carry hairs. The actual blooms are yellowish and very small. Shining, purple red, oval-tapered bracts surround each three of them. There are cultivars with varying colours.

SITE:

For aesthetic purposes, canalized riverbeds in Funchal and Santa Cruz are covered with wires on which are growing Bougainvillea plants. They also grow on other sites and are among the most popular ornamental plants on Madeira for their abundance of flowers. Up to an altitude of 450 m (490 yd.) and especially in the south you can find them nearly everywhere.

INTERESTING TO KNOW:

Although to a smaller extent, the similar Great Bougainvillea (Bougainvillea spectabilis) is also cultivated on Madeira. It has hairy leaves and purple-red, heart-shaped petals. Crossbreeding of the two species allowed to develop specimens of various colours (purple, pink, orange, white). The botanical denomination reminds of the French navigator Louis Antoine de Bougainville. The Bougainvilleas were discovered on an excursion to Brazil 1766-1769 that was led by him.

GOLD CUP, CHALICE VINE
SOLANDRA MAXIMA

BLOOM TIME

All year round, except summer.

CHARACTERISTICS

The woody climber plant reaches up to 12 m (13 yd.) tall. The leathery leaves are elliptical and short-tapered. A very conspicuous feature are the yellow, funnel-shaped flowers. The calyx is curved outwards to form a broad, five-lobed hem. A purple-brown ridge runs into the centre of the funnel.

SITE:

As it grows very tall in a short time, the plant is mostly cultivated in larger gardens and parks. On Madeira you will often see it in the south, up to an altitude of 350 m (385 yd.). There are for example several specimens to be found in Funchal in the park of the Quinta Vigia or in the Botanical Garden.

INTERESTING TO KNOW:

The Gold Cup is native to the American tropics. The still closed buds contain water that is used there by traditional medicine to treat conjunctivitis. However, the plant itself is poisonous. The Indians used it for the production of intoxicating drugs. In nature, Gold Cup is pollinated by bats. Thus the blossoms open in the evening - and that fast that you can watch them developing. Another typical characteristic for flowers that attract bats is the mawkish scent that is much more intense during night hours.

GOLDEN SHOWER, ORANGE TRUMPET VINE
PYROSTEGIA VENUSTA

BLOOM TIME
From November to February.

CHARACTERISTICS
This climber develops up to 10 m (11 yd.) long shoots. The leaves are mostly organized threefold; they are elliptic to longish with a lopsided basis. At the bottom, the leaves are covered with red-brown hairs. The shining blossoms hang down in dense panicles that reach up to 6 cm (2,5") long and resemble tubes or funnels.

SITE:
On Madeira, the Golden Shower is most likely to be cultivated on walls, fences and pergolas. It grows mainly in the south of the island, up to an altitude of about 350 m (385 yd.). You will often find it both in private gardens and in public parks (e.g. Botanical Garden, Funchal).

INTERESTING TO KNOW:
The Golden Shower is native to Brazil. Nowadays it is cultivated globally in tropical and subtropical countries. Golden Shower is part of the Bignonia family (Bignoniaceae). The Cape Honeysuckle (Tecomaria capensis), plant native to South Africa, which blossoms all year round, is as well assigned to this group. You can also find this poorly climbing shrub being cultivated on Madeira, often next to the Golden Shower. Its leaves are organized in groups of 6-9; its blossoms are also forming dense panicles. They grow upright and open to showy funnels.

Mexican Bread fruit
Monstera deliciosa

Bloom time
From June to September.

Characteristics

Branches of this climber can be more than 10 m (11 yd.) tall and develop numerous aerial roots. The giant leaves are firstly heart-shaped, later they become perforated with holes or pinnately lobed. The cream-coloured spadix is up to 25 cm (10") long and half covered with a thick, white bract.

Site:
In the south of Madeira you will frequently see the Mexican Bread Fruit in various parks and private gardens up to an altitude of 400 m (440 yd.). You can for example encounter it in the Jardim Municipal and in the Botanical Garden in Funchal. It does not only climb along trees but also along walls and fences.

Interesting to know:
The plant is native to Mexico. In summer, the plant develops an edible spadix out of each inflorescence. In Portugal, this fruit is called "fruto delicioso" (delicious fruit) and valued as a delicacy. The spadix consists of numerous fleshy, hexagonal cells that mature little by little from the bottom to the top. The taste ranges between a banana and a pineapple. Nevertheless you have to take care: the fruit contains oxalic acid that might cause irritations of the mucous membrances. On the market in Funchal the fruits are offered to the tourist for tidy prices.

Fan Aloe
Aloe plicatilis

Bloom time
April and May.

Characteristics

The plant only grows up to 2 m (6,6') tall but develops a thick trunk from which emerge numerous branches with a crest of long, fleshy, grey-green leaves at the end of each. The leaves are organized in two opposite files. The red racemes resemble pointed cones and grow upright on thin stalks.

Site:
The Fan Aloe origins from South Africa. In the south of Madeira it is cultivated up to an altitude of 400 m (440 yd.) and decorates both private gardens and parks. Some especially beautiful specimens are growing in the succulent plants section in the Botanical Garden in Funchal.

Interesting to know:
The Fan Aloe was already introduced to Europe in the 17th century and since then has been very popular as a container plant. Outdoors it only flourishes all year round in habitats without any frost. Together with Barbados Aloe, the Fan Aloe counts among the species from which aloe resin is extracted. The resin is produced by squeezing the sap from the leaves and thickening it. Mixed with sulphuric acid the aloe resin can be employed as dye. Occasionally it is still used as a laxative. For this effect it was indispensable in former times when defecation was the basis of every medical treatment.

SWORD ALOE
ALOE ARBORESCENS

BLOOM TIME

From October to February.

CHARACTERISTICS

The slender, fleshy leaves have serrated margins. They are organized in dense rosettes with a diameter of about 50 cm (20"). Several rosettes are situated on each of the short, branched trunks. Long stalks with various cone-shaped, shining red flowers emerge out of every rosette.

SITE:

In the southern coastal regions the Sword Aloe is one of the most popular ornamental plants lining the roadsides (up to an altitude of 600 m (656 yd.), although mostly on a lower level). It is often cultivated in gardens, parks and around special points of view. Sometimes it becomes wild in fallow land.

INTERESTING TO KNOW:

The Sword Aloe is native to South Africa. The remaining 200 Aloe species are also originating from Africa, Madagascar and Arabia. Although on the first sight you may observe a striking similarity with Agaves, the two genera are only distant relatives. The latter's habitat is restricted on the regions between the south of the U. S. A. and South America. Anyway, both genera were lead independently to similar adaptations and to a similar outer appearance by comparable living conditions in interim habitats between savannah and desert (thorn bush savannah).

Bear's Breech
Acanthus mollis

Bloom time
From May to July.

Characteristics

The herbal plant develops candle-shaped inflorescences that grow up to 1 m (3,3') tall. The tongue-shaped single blooms are whitish with purple veins. The superior lobe of the calyx is remarkably enlarged. The large, dark green leaves are strongly lobed and have substantial leaf veins.

Site:
You will mostly find Bear's Breech in gardens in the south of the island, up to an altitude of 600 m (655 yd.). It often grows wild along streets or levadas. You can see numerous specimens in the Palheiro Gardens at the entrance to the Camellia Avenue. You will also encounter it in Camacha.

Interesting to know:
The Bear's Breech is native to the Mediterranean region and Asia Minor. As those of the Spiny Bear's Breech (Acanthus spinosus), its leaves served as models for the ornaments at the pillar capitals of the Corinthian temple in ancient Greek. Later this symbol of fertility was taken over by the Romans. Since the 15th century it has been picked up again and again in European architecture. On Madeira you may often find it in form of ceramic sculptures on the corners of old houses' tiled roofs. They symbolize the large number of children that shall be bestowed upon the family.

ROSEA ICE PLANT
DROSANTHEMUM FLORIBUNDUM

BLOOM TIME
From April to July.

CHARACTERISTICS

The plant has numerous little, fleshy leaves that are placed on thin stalks. In their natural habitat these stalks use to lie on the ground. However, the plant is mostly cultivated as a hanging plant. The blooms have a bright centre, which is surrounded by a wreath of narrow, purple petals.

SITE:
On Madeira, the Rosea Ice Plant is mostly culti-vated in private gardens up to an altitude of 800 m (875 yd.), although in the north of the island you will not find it in that high regions. It is frequently planted on balconies or along walls. You may also see it growing in hanging baskets.
INTERESTING TO KNOW:
The Rosea Ice Plant is native to South Africa, as is the similar Red Midday Flower (Carpobrotus acinaciformis). The latter has very large blos-soms and thick, fleshy leaves and is planted on Madeira both in gardens and along walls. Although it is also just an "introduced" plant it is known as "the" Midday Flower the Mediter-ranean. Midday Flowers in its narrower sense are part of the genus Mesembryanthemum. Two of its species are wildly growing on Ma-deira (cf. p. 81). It is a common characteristic of all Midday Flowers that they only open their blossoms in sunshine and around noon.

WHITE BIRD OF PARADISE, NATAL WILD BANANA STRELITZIA NICOLAI

BLOOM TIME
All year round.

CHARACTERISTICS

With its tree-like growth and its long leaves the White Bird of Paradise resembles a banana plant. However, the leaves are organized in two opposite ranks. Each inflorescence is composed by up to five single blossoms that all have a similar structure to those of the Crane Flower (cf. p. 49).

SITE:
On Madeira, the White Bird of Paradise is mostly growing in parks and gardens in Funchal. It prefers warm, sheltered and well-moistured sites. Beautiful specimen plants are to be found among others in the Parque Santa Catarina and in the Quinta das Cruzes.

INTERESTING TO KNOW:
The White Bird of Paradise is native to South Africa where it grows from the eastern Cape through Natal and Mozambique to Zimbabwe. Among the five species of the genus Strelitzia, the Crane Flower is the only one that maintains low. The remaining four can reach up to tree-like dimensions. Despite of its height and the thick trunk, the White Bird of the Paradise is not a tree. The trunk is not made out of wood but of stalks that are widened at the bottom. Similar to those of the related banana, the tender stalks of Natal Wild Banana mainly consist of water.

CRANE FLOWER,
BIRD OF PARADISE FLOWER
STRELITZIA REGINAE

BLOOM TIME

All year round, mainly in winter and spring.

CHARACTERISTICS

The leaves resemble those of a banana plant but are placed on long stalks that emerge directly from the rhizome. On the long blossom stalks are situated beak-shaped sheaths from which develop up to three flowers. The petals are 10 cm (4") long; three are narrow and orange, three spit-like and purple.

SITE:

The Crane Flower is frequently cultivated in Madeira's parks and gardens. It prefers the south of the island up to an altitude of 400 m (440 yd.). Here and there it may also be planted on fields for commercial purposes. A border of these attractive plants is to be found in the Botanical Garden in Funchal.

INTERESTING TO KNOW:

The plant is indigenous to the Cape of Good Hope. Its botanical denomination is due to the German botanist and gardener Andreas Auge who was in service to the British East Indian Company and founded the Botanical Garden in Cape Town that is worldwide recognized today. He wanted to honour Charlotte of Mecklenburg-Strelitz (Strelitzia), spouse of King George III, on the occasion of the Kings' visit to Cape Town in 1774. Under favourable conditions you can keep the cut flower in blossom for nearly two weeks.

INDIAN SHOT
CANNA INDICA

BLOOM TIME
From April to October.

CHARACTERISTICS
The stalks and the broad, greenish-purple leaves are forming a sham trunk of about 1 m (3,3') height from which emerges a blossom stalk. On the latter is placed a panicle that is composed by ten completely asymmetrical blossoms. The wild form has narrow, red petals; cultivars may be orange, pink and white.

SITE:
The Indian Shot is mostly seen in the coastal regions. Anyway it grows up to an altitude of 700 m (765 yd.) in the south of the island. It is a popular horticulture plant. It often propagates vegetatively by root shoots; thus you can see it growing in larger groups. As in the public garden at the central square of Camacha, it is used to decorate flower borders in parks. A large population is to be found in the "Inferno" in the Palheiro Gardens.

INTERESTING TO KNOW:
The botanical denomination of the genus reminds of the similarity to cane. They also share a similar habitat. In their natural habitat in South America, Canna species grow at riverbanks, along lakes and swamps. Thus the Indian Shot is not native to India but to the tropical American regions ("West India"). On Madeira you can find both its wild form and various cultivars.

SPLENDID CYMBIDIUM
CYMBIDIUM INSIGNE

BLOOM TIME
From January to May.

CHARACTERISTICS
This conspicuous orchid develops a raceme of 50-100 cm (20-40") length with up to 25 large flowers. The single blossoms are bilaterally symmetrical with five petals and a broad lip in the centre. The flower uses to be pale pink with a purple spotted lip.

SITE:
On Madeira, Splendid Cymbidium is grown up to an altitude of 500 m (550 yd.). Planted in pots it decorates balconies, terraces and outside staircases of many houses mainly in the island's north. In the drier south it is most often planted under gauze nets to protect it from sun and wind. Among other sites you can find a wide range of various Cymbidiums and other orchids in the Quinta da Boa Vista in Funchal. Smaller orchid sections are to be explored in the Quinta das Cruzes and in the Botanical Garden.

INTERESTING TO KNOW:
Splendid Cymbidium is native to Vietnam. In contrast to the majority of epiphyte orchids (tree orchids) it is growing on the ground. In Europe you may cultivate it indoors or outdoors during the summer season. It prefers bright and breezy sites and is recognized for its long bloom time. On Madeira you find Splendid Cymbidium being cultivated on various flower farms.

Red Hot Poker
Kniphofia uvaria

Bloom time

From March to September.

Characteristics

This species of the Lily family grows up to 1 m (3,3') tall and has long, narrow, basal leaves and erect blossom stalks. A torch-shaped raceme is placed on each of them. The tubular flowers blossom gradually from the bottom to the top. In an early stage they are coloured orange, before wilting they become yellow.

Site:
You will encounter Red Hot Poker in all coastal areas. In the south it grows up to an altitude of 700 m (765 yd.). You can find it in the Botanical Garden in Funchal. Grown in flower borders it decorates many parks and private gardens.

Interesting to know:
The plant is indigenous to South Africa. Already in the 18th century it was introduced to Europe where it can even be grown outdoors under moderate climatic conditions. The denomination of the genus commemorates J. H. Kniphof (1704-1763), professor at Erfurt university (Germany). The grape-like plant became a popular garden plant primarily in the Netherlands and in the Anglo-Saxon countries. It was cross-bred with some of other 70 known Kniphofia species. Today there are known more than 150 hybrids. Many more were lost during the Second World War when by law British flower gardens had to be replaced by vegetable fields.

BIG FLAMINGO FLOWER
ANTHURIUM ANDREANUM

BLOOM TIME
All year round.

CHARACTERISTICS
The broad, dark leaves have a heart-like basis and a tapered tip. The stalks emerge directly from the rhizome, as also does the blossom stalk. It becomes up to 80 cm (32") long and bears a giant flower that consists of a yellow spadix and a large, red spathe. There are cultivars in white or pink.

SITE:
On Madeira you will see the Big Flamingo Flower growing up to an altitude of 500 m (550 yd.). It needs a humid, sheltered site and is often cultivated below gauze nets to protect it from direct sunlight. In Funchal you can find Big Flamingo Flower for example in the Quinta das Cruzes in the orchid section or in the Botanical Garden. In many private gardens it is planted in pots next to the house. Flowers are sold to market traders.

INTERESTING TO KNOW:
The Big Flamingo Flower is native to Columbia. Apart from this species you can also find the Flamingo Flower/Pigtail Plant being cultivated on Madeira, a similar, but harder species. Anyway, the latter is quite rare. It only grows up to 40 cm (16") high and has a red spadix and an equally red, but narrower spathe. Its leaves are longish. Wild forms of both species are growing as epiphytes in their native habitats.

CAPE CHINCHERINCHEE, AFRICAN WONDER FLOWER ORNITHOGALUM THYRSOIDES

BLOOM TIME
May and June.

CHARACTERISTICS
This bulb plant develops up to 60 cm (24") high, erect blossom stalks that carry pointed cone-shaped inflorescences. The single blossoms are milky-white on the inside and resemble little stars for its pointed petals. The narrow, long leaves emerge from rosettes at the stalk's basis.

SITE:
In altitudes of 200-800 m (220-875 yd.) you may often find the Cape Chincherinchee growing in gardens and parks in the south of the island. It is especially frequent in Camacha where it is cultivated on little fields for the selling of cut flowers on the flower markets in Funchal.

INTERESTING TO KNOW:
The Cape Chincherinchee belongs to the Lily family. It is indigenous to South Africa where it is highly frequent in the Cape region. The living conditions there are quite similar to those of the Mediterranean, the habitat of various species related to Cape Chincherinchee. With the Star of Bethlehem (Ornithogalum umbellatum) there is even one species growing in Central Europe. All Ornithogalum species have similar blossoms and are thus difficult to distinguish. The most obvious difference uses to be the shape of the inflorescences. Within the European species they are of a much looser form.

BARBADOS LILY, AMARYLLIS
HIPPEASTRUM VITTATUM

BLOOM TIME
From March to May.

CHARACTERISTICS
The Barbados Lily is very popular as an ornamental plant. It is related to narcissuses and has the typical long and narrow leaves. Several blossoms are placed together at the top of thick stems. The colour ranges from pale pink to dark red. The six petals with central stripes are not grown together.

SITE:
On Madeira Barbados Lily is a pure garden plant; in contrast to the similar Belladonna Lily (cf. p. 110) you will thus never find it in a wild form. Barbados Lily is most often cultivated in big parks at average altitudes: in the Botanical Garden, in the Palheiro Gardens, in the Jardim Tropical Monte Palace. Even in the north of the island you may find it quite often in private gardens.

INTERESTING TO KNOW:
The Barbados Lily, primarily its pink cultivars, is easily mixed up with the on Madeira much more frequent Belladonna Lily. The latter blossoms in autumn; its petals are grown together and form a funnel. Worldwide the Barbados Lily, native to South America, is the most often cultivated "Amaryllis". Anyway, botanists have disembodied it from this genus. Today the Belladonna Lily is the only "true" Amaryllis.

NOBLE NATAL LILY
CLIVIA NOBILIS

BLOOM TIME
From July to November.

CHARACTERISTICS

The plant becomes up to 50 cm (20") tall and is part of the Amaryllis family. The light green, up to 90 cm (35") long leaves emerge directly from the rhizome and form a basic rosette. The flower stems raise little above the leaves and carry umbels of up to 15 shining orange-red, funnel-shaped single blossoms at their tip.

SITE:
On Madeira, Nobal Natal Lily is cultivated up to an altitude of 500 m (550 yd.). It prospers well in the shadow of high trees and prefers certain humidity. You will find it in many gardens and nearly all parks.

INTERESTING TO KNOW:
As the more frequent Small Natal Lily (Clivia minata), Noble Natal Lily originates from South Africa. Small Natal Lily has shorter leaves and erect, wider opened blossoms that appear from April to June. They are coloured strongly orange with a yellow centre in the blossom's funnel. It also prefers moist, sheltered sites and is for example to be found in the Jardim Tropical Monte Palace. Clivias were introduced to Europe in 1854 and named in honour of Lady C. Clive, Duchess of Northumberland. In those days they had strap-like leaves. Through various breedings they have been widened to make the plant more attractive.

CAPE COAST LILY
CRINUM POWELLII

BLOOM TIME
From December to May.

CHARACTERISTICS
The up to 50 cm (20") tall perennial develops strong, long leaves that dry out in winter. An umbel of various large, white or pale pink coloured, funnel-shaped blooms is situated atop of the flower stem. Each blossom consists of five petals. The flowers stick out sideways or even hang down.

SITE:
The Cape Coast Lily prefers moist, sheltered sites. As an ornamental plant it is often grown under trees in gardens and parks. You will see it frequently; sometimes it is even employed to line paths and roadsides especially in the more humid north of the island. It does not have any tendency to go wild.

INTERESTING TO KNOW:
The plant is botanically related to the Clivias and belongs to the Amaryllis family. Close relatives are the Belladonna Lily (cf. p. 110) and the Barbados Lily (cf. p. 55). Containing more than 100 species, the genus Crinum is spread worldwide through all tropical and subtropical regions, especially in coastal areas or generally close to water. The Cape Coast Lily is a crossbreeding between the South African species Crinum bulbispermum and Crinum moorei. Thus it is a pure garden plant.

VEGETATION IN COASTAL AREAS

The climate of Madeira's southern coastal area resembles the climate of the Mediterranean region. The summers are relatively hot and dry; rainfalls are mainly restricted to the time from October to May. These months are characterised by a mild spring climate. It is probable that a certain type of scrubland, similar to the Mediterranean Macchia, populated the south of the island up to an altitude of about 300 m (330 yd.) when the Portuguese settled on Madeira in the 15th century. It was composed of Dragon Trees, Canary Junipers and Madeiran Wild Olive Trees. The Smooth Spear-leaved Spurge, the Splendid Viper's Bugloss and other bushes thrived on steep slopes that are hardly ever populated by trees because of constant soil erosion.

In spring, numerous endemic herbs and perennials converted the southern, sun-rich coastal areas in a flowering sea. Many of these plants are succulent, i.e. they store water in their leaves or stalks for the dry season and for avoiding to receive too much salt from the soil.

Others only sprout in the more humid winter months and withdraw their overhead organs in the dry season. In the wetter and chillier north of the island you will only find a comparable flora in the immediate vicinity of the coast.

At many places men replaced the natural coastal vegetation with settlements and sugar cane plantations, later with banana plantations. Tropical trees and shrubs were cultivated in flower gardens. As sugar cane and bananas they can only survive under these relatively dry conditions with the help of artificial watering. The required water is conducted by levadas (cf. p. 87) from more humid areas mainly in the north of the island. The native shrubland has remained fairly unchanged at only a few sites that are mostly located in nearly inaccessible areas (e.g. slopes of the valley of Ribeira Brava, steep coasts between Funchal and Garajau). Shrubs and smaller plants that are part of the coastal vegetation are to be found at many sites on fallow land or along roadsides.

The most eastern part of Madeira, the peninsula São Lourenço, is part of the island's Natural Park entirely under conservation today. Prohibitions to enter certain grounds and new plantings should help to regenerate the coastal vegetation. A popular trail crosses this area. The coastal landscapes of Ribeira do Tristão (below Achadas da Cruz) and Rocha do Navio (close to Santana) that can only be reached by a funicular or by steep trails are also under conservation. The Ponta São Lourenço is especially worthy of visiting in March/April. May is the main bloom time in the two remaining natural reserves in the north of the island.

CANARY ISLAND DATE PALM
PHOENIX CANARIENSIS

BLOOM TIME
From January to March

CHARACTERISTICS
This palm grows up to 20 m (22 yd.) tall. It resembles the True Date Palm (Phoenix dactylifera) but has a thicker trunk and a dense crown. The fronds can be 5-6 m (5,5-6,5 yd.) long. The brownish inflorescences are inconspicuous. The orange fruits are small (ca. 2 cm/ 0,8") and only slightly fleshy.

SITE:
On Madeira, the Canary Island Date Palm grows in coastal areas up to an altitude of 400 m (440 yd.). On the peninsula São Lourenço it lines the old street that leads to Caniçal. Hikers will encounter it in the "oasis" at the most eastern point of the island. It is also to be found along promenades and in parks.

INTERESTING TO KNOW:
The Canary Island Date Palm is endemic to the Canary Islands. It is a fast growing plant and quite tolerant of cold; thus and for its showy appearance it has been introduced to Madeira and to all Mediterranean regions. The dates are inedible for human beings. They were used as pig feed in earlier times. The plant contains a sap that is tapped on the Canary Islands and processed to produce a palm honey that is used for various desserts. This custom has never been adapted on Madeira.

DRAGON TREE,
DRAGON'S BLOOD TREE
DRACAENA DRACO

BLOOM TIME

All 10-15 years in August and September.

CHARACTERISTICS

The branches emerge in determined distances from a thick trunk. Rosettes of long, narrow leaves are placed at the tips of the youngest twigs. In contrast to the inconspicuous inflorescences, the poisonous berries are shining orange. On Madeira, the largest Dragon Trees are about 6 m (6,5 yd.) tall.

SITE:

By nature, the Dragon Tree used to be quite frequent in the drier coastal areas. Today it is nearly extinct in that area. You can find two wild growing specimens at a rock face east of Ribeira Brava; a little colony survived in São Gonçalo close to Funchal. The tree is often cultivated in parks and there are attempts to reintroduce it to the peninsula São Lourenço, above the Prainha.

INTERESTING TO KNOW:

Already in the 14th century the first dealers came to Madeira to tap the dragon's blood (the resin) and to produce a natural red dye out of it. Thus the tree was already nearly extinct at the end of the 16th century. Similar happenings took place on the Canary Islands and Cape Verde Islands. The Dragon Trees on Tenerife were long time popular for their believed age of more than thousand years. Dragon Trees do not develop annual rings but it is known today they can reach a maximum of 400 years.

MADEIRA WILD OLIVE TREE
OLEA EUROPAEA MADERENSIS

BLOOM TIME

May and June, fruit bearing from November to January.

CHARACTERISTICS

The shrub or small tree is about 3 m (10') tall and more filigree than the popular Common Olive Tree. The narrow leaves are pointed, grey-green on the surface and whitish at the bottom. They are leathery and thus well protected against evaporation. The black, 1 cm (0,4") long fruits develop from the blooms.

SITE:
You will mostly find the Madeira Wild Olive Tree at steep, inaccessible slopes in the south of the island. Up to an altitude of 500 m (547 yd.) it grows at sites with well-preserved, natural coastal vegetation. You can e.g. encounter it at the slopes of the lower valley of Ribeira Brava or along the coast between Funchal and Caniço. Close to Caniço de Baixo a headland is named after it (Ponta da Oliveira).

INTERESTING TO KNOW:
The cultivated form of Olive Tree is supposed to originate from Persia and the Caucasus. On Madeira you will not encounter this much mightier tree with its broader, shorter leaves outside the parks. Only in Caniçal there are a few specimens lining the road to the Praia Ribeira de Natal. There you can find some people who still pick olives. Nevertheless, these olives are small and taste bitter. Olives that are sold on the markets come from the Portuguese mainland.

FRENCH TAMARISK
TAMARIX GALLICA

BLOOM TIME
From January to August

CHARACTERISTICS
The shrub or small tree (2-4 m/6,6-13") is a multi-branched flowering plant with sparsely green foliage. The small, grey-green leaves are placed like scales at the end of tender twigs. They remind of conifers. The white to pink coloured inflorescences resemble willow catkins.

SITE:
French Tamarisk grows most frequently at rocky sites close to the coast or next to river mouths that are dried out most of the year. To a certain amount it tolerates saline soils. It never grows at altitudes higher than 200 m (220 yd.). You can easily find it along the promenade in Porto Moniz or on the headland of Porto da Cruz. It has recently been cultivated on the peninsula Ponta São Lourenço to prevent erosion.

INTERESTING TO KNOW:
The Canary Islands and the Cape Verde Islands are the natural habitat of the Canary Island Tamarisk (Tamarix canariensis). This species was earlier regarded as a subspecies of the French Tamarisk which is spread in the Mediterranean region. Until now scientists still assign the Madeiran variation to the genus Tamarix gallica. It is said that the plant was introduced as a timber in ancient times.

COASTAL AREAS

CASTOR-OIL PLANT
RICINUS COMMUNIS

BLOOM TIME
All year round

CHARACTERISTICS

The shrub is 1-3 m (3,3-10")
tall. A typical feature are the
hand-shaped leaves with up
to nine "fingers". Twigs and
leaf veins are reddish. The
thick, spadix-shaped inflorescences develop female
blooms at the top and males
at the bottom. The females
produce the prickly fruits.

SITE:
Up to an altitude of 400 m (440 yd.), the Castor-
Oil Plant grows wild in all coastal areas of the
island. You will most frequently encounter it
on wasteland within villages: on development
land, on abandoned land and along roadsides.

INTERESTING TO KNOW:
Growing out of the seed the plant can reach
its full height in the course of only a few
months; thus it is also commonly known as
"Wonder Tree". Already the ancient Egyptians
were familiar with the Castor-Oil Plant.
Today it has spread in nearly all tropical and
subtropical countries. The fruits contain the
castor oil. In former times it was used as a
laxative or as a lighting agent. Today it serves
as a lubricant for aeroplanes and ships, as a
brake fluid and as a softening agent in plastic
production. The seeds are very poisonous: only
three or four seeds can be lethal for children.

SPLENDID VIPER'S BUGLOSS
ECHIUM NERVOSUM

BLOOM TIME
From January to April

CHARACTERISTICS
The broad shrub is up to 1 m (3,3") tall and develops numerous, upright growing twigs that are covered with a multitude of sharp, bluish-green leaves and carry attractive, candle-like, pale blue to purple inflorescences at the tip. These are rounded off and thus seem to be compressed.

SITE:
The Splendid Viper's Bugloss is restricted to coastal areas where it grows at dry slopes, in the north only up an altitude of 100 m (110 yd.), in the south up to 300 m (330 yd.). You can for example find it quite frequently above the old northwest coastal road between Seixal and Porto Moniz or along the motorway that connects the airport with Funchal. Hikers encounter it in the nature reserve Ribeira do Tristão (close to Achadas da Cruz). It is also grown as an ornamental plant along roadsides or on traffic islands.

INTERESTING TO KNOW:
In contrast to the Purple Viper's Bugloss (cf. p. 76), Splendid Viper's Bugloss is endemic to Madeira. It is mostly pollinated by bumblebees, which you can easily observe on the inflorescences. Very rarely it can be pollinated by the endemic Madeira Lizard. This hardly timid animal feeds on nectar and fruits.

65

WILLOWLIKE GLOBE FLOWER
GLOBULARIA SALICINA

BLOOM TIME
From March to December

CHARACTERISTICS

The 1 m (3,3') shrub grows spherically. The narrow, sharp leaves resemble those of a willow and are placed spirally around the twigs. The genus denomination refers to the numerous global inflorescences. They are about 1 cm (0,4") in diameter and situated on short stalks among the leaves.

SITE:
In the south, the Willowlike Globe Flower grows up to an altitude of 400 m (440 yd.), in the north only up to 100 m (110 yd.). Together with the similarly growing Smooth Spear-leaved Spurge (cf. p. 67) it founds large populations at steep, unspoiled slopes.

INTERESTING TO KNOW:
The Willowlike Globe Flower is endemic to Madeira and the Canary Islands. Two smaller species are restricted to Grand Canary. All other species (around 30) that belong to the genus Globularia are native to the Mediterranean regions and the Alps. In contrast to the Willowlike Globe Flower, they are mostly flowering strong blue, have larger capitulas and are of herbaceous growth (like a "flower"). The leaves of all species contain globularin, a resin with laxative effects. They are employed to treat constipation by popular medicine.

SMOOTH SPEAR-LEAVED SPURGE
EUPHORBIA PISCATORIA

BLOOM TIME
From January to August, mostly in April/May

CHARACTERISTICS
Although the shrub can grow up to 2 m (6,6') tall, the average height is 1 m (3,3'). It is extremely ramified and has inconspicuous, yellowish flowers. The narrow, blue to green leaves are shed off in spring. New leaves will sprout in autumn, right after the first heavy rainfalls.

SITE:
The Smooth Spear-eaved Spurge is the most typical plant of Madeira's drought-preferring coastal vegetation. It often creates dense undergrowth on unspoiled slopes. In the south it grows up to an altitude of 300 m (330 yd.), in the north only up to 100 m (110 yd.) .

INTERESTING TO KNOW:
All parts of the plant contain a toxic milky sap. The botanical denomination refers to the fact that in former times the inhabitants of the coastal areas used this sap for fishing. Mostly in the north of the island the sea used to be too rough to allow little boats to put out to sea. Thus the fishers waited until the high tide would drive shoals of fishes into the tide ponds. They anaesthetized the fishes with the milky sap and could then gather them up. It is supposed that in the 15th century, slaves from the Canary Islands introduced this fishing method to Madeira.

ELEPHANT EAR PRICKLY PEAR
OPUNTIA FICUS-INDICA

BLOOM TIME
From June to September

CHARACTERISTICS
The prickly shrub grows up to 1,5 m (5') tall. The stalks are green, fleshy and flat. The single links are ovate in reverse and replace the very receded leaves. The flowers are of a shining orange colour and develop into prickly, 5-10 cm (2-4") long fruits.

SITE:
Up to an altitude of 400 m (440 yd.), the Elephant Ear Prickly Pear grows frequently at the coastal slopes in the south of the island. The largest populations are to be found between Funchal and Caniço and around Ribeira Brava.

INTERESTING TO KNOW:
The Elephant Ear Prickly Pear is indigenous to Mexico. Already in the 16th century it was introduced to Madeira for its edible fruits. Up to now the ripe fruits are harvested in September and sold by fruit dealers on the streets of Funchal. The harvest is supervised by the municipalities in charge: they allocate licences and impose taxes on each basket. On several plants you may observe a whitish, felty film. In fact, you see cochineal insects. Before artificial colours were invented they provided a valuable red dye. Anyway, attempts in the 19th century to produce dye for the export failed.

WILD ARTICHOKE, PRICKLY CARDOON
CYNARA CARDUNCULUS

BLOOM TIME

From July to October, partly in March

CHARACTERISTICS

The long, prickly leaves form a dense rosette. Compound flowers develop from the up to 45 cm (18") long stalks. The flowers consist of several purple, tubular blossoms. They lack the widened bottom that is typical for cultivated artichokes.

SITE:

The Wild Artichoke grows exclusively at arid, sunny sites in coastal areas, mainly at 50-100 m (55-110 yd.) altitude on profound soils that are rich in nutrients. Animals scorn this prickly plant. Thus it is very frequent on the peninsula São Lourenço where large areas have been used as pastureland in earlier days.

INTERESTING TO KNOW:

Besides Madeira, the Wild Artichoke is indigenous to the Canary Islands and the Mediterranean region. Probably it is the wild progenitor of Globe Artichoke (Cynara scolymus), a species that only occurs in cultivation and was already planted in ancient Egypt. The bleached flower stalks of the wild form are eaten in Mediterranean regions. After bloom time the leaves are tied into bunches and covered with straw. They can be harvested three weeks later. The Madeiran form is especially prickly; thus it will not be picked up here.

COASTAL AREAS

DOWNY SOW THISTLE
ANDRYALA GLANDULOSA

BLOOM TIME
From April to August

CHARACTERISTICS

This compound flower is up to 30 cm (12") tall. Its inflorescences consist of various, golden-yellow blossoms that resemble those of dandelions. The whitish leaves have slightly upwards curved margins and are organized in rosettes. Both leaves and stalks are extremely sticky.

SITE:
The Downy Sow Thistle prefers rocks in coastal areas up to an altitude of 200 m (220 yd.). Hikers can for example find it on the peninsula Ponta São Lourenço. It is difficult to distinguish from the Variable Sow Thistle (Andryala varia). The latter grows at average altitudes and even reaches up to the mountains. As it is already indicated by the name, this species contains various forms. The leaves are up to 20 cm (8") long and not that sticky. The plant can grow up to 0,5 m (1,6") tall. Some botanists classify it as a subspecies of the Downy Sow Thistle.

INTERESTING TO KNOW:
The genus Andryala contains many species. Botanists described various species and subspecies that are endemic to the Atlantic Islands. Anyway, it is often difficult to differentiate among them down to the last detail. The sticky excretions of many tender glandular hairs function as a trap to protect the plant against pests.

70

MADEIRA MING FERN
ASPARAGUS UMBELLATUS

BLOOM TIME

Quite short bloom time from November to January

CHARACTERISTICS

The climber can develop up to 5 m (5,5 yd.) long trunks. The leaves are receded to inconspicuous scales. Green, needle-like, short sprouts that are grouped in tufts and placed on the twigs replace them. The white flowers form umbels. The berries are yellowish.

SITE:

Madeira Ming Fern grows wild on rocky slopes at the northern coast where it creeps around trees. It is quite rare. You will most easily encounter it in the Botanical Garden or in a park.

INTERESTING TO KNOW:

This species is also growing on all Canary Islands except for Lanzarote. The Esparto Asparagus (Asparagus scoparius) is another species that is endemic to Madeira, the Canary Islands and the Cape Verde Islands. Anyway, the latter is not a climbing plant and prefers dry sites in coastal areas. The young sprouts of Madeira's wild asparagus species are not eaten, neither are cultivated vegetable forms of this genus. Only a few years ago imported European asparagus has been introduced to Madeiran supermarkets.

COMMON FENNEL
FOENICULUM VULGARE

BLOOM TIME
From July to September

CHARACTERISTICS

The 50-100 cm (20-40") tall plant has finely pinnate, aromatic leaves. During bloom time it develops various long, nearly bleak stalks with plate-shaped umbels. The single blossoms are quite inconspicuous and yellowish. The entire plant resembles dill.

SITE:
Common Fennel frequently grows on fallow land up to an altitude of 400 m (440 yd.). Among other sites you can encounter it at Cape Garajau, at the Miradouro do Pico (close to Ribeira Brava), around the lighthouse of Ponta do Pargo and in the region of Porto da Cruz. You may also find it at more humid sites, for example along the Levada do Central above Porto Moniz.

INTERESTING TO KNOW:
The Portuguese word for fennel is funcho. It is said that in the 15th century the first settlers encountered wild growing Common Fennel in the bay of Funchal. Thus the city got its current name which means, liberally translated, "fennel meadow". The plant contains ethereal oil that was traditionally employed by the Madeirans for the production of cough sweets. They taste quite bitter. The orange "fennel sweets" that are sold in gift shops today are aromatised with sweeter aniseed.

DYER'S WOAD
ISATIS TINCTORIA

BLOOM TIME
From March to May

CHARACTERISTICS

Dyer's Woad belongs to the Mustard family and resembles rape, a related species. Including the inflorescence, the plant is 30-70 cm (12-28") tall. The small, yellow flowers are grouped in numerous, dense racemes. The bluish-green leaves clasp the stalk like an arrow.

SITE:
Dyer's Woad prefers warmer sites and is to be found in coastal areas up to an altitude of 200 m (220 yd.), especially on the peninsula São Lourenço. You can also encounter it in the western city zone of Funchal, below the Cabo Girão, around Fajã dos Padres and Ribeira Brava.

INTERESTING TO KNOW:
Dyer's Woad is indigenous to Southeast Europe and West Asia. It contains the toxic natural dye indigo blue and was thus cultivated in Europe for about 2000 years up to the 19th century. To extract the colour the herb needs to be cut and fermented. In the 15th century the Portuguese introduced Dyer's Woad to Madeira to produce dye. It was exported to Italy and Flanders until the 16th century. The plant lost its importance in the 17th century when imports from India introduced the authentic, more productive indigo to Europe. The Dyer's Woad went wild and is widespread today on Madeira.

CORN POPPY
PAPAVER RHOEAS

BLOOM TIME
From March to May

CHARACTERISTICS

Corn Poppy is known throughout the Mediterranean region. On Madeira it inhabits arid sites and only reaches up to an altitude of 200 m (220 yd.). The big, red flowers consist of four petals and are placed individually on thin stalks. The plant contains a toxic milky sap.

SITE:
The Corn Poppy grows in coastal areas, for example on the peninsula São Lourenço or in the natural reserve of Ribeira do Tristão near to Achadas da Cruz. Most of the time you will only encounter specimen plants. Anyway, for their shining colour they will definitely attract your attention.

INTERESTING TO KNOW:
You can find various Poppy species on Madeira. The most conspicuous species is the Bristly Poppy (Papaver setigerum). It populates the same sites that are settled by the Corn Poppy but is easily distinguished by its pale pink flowers. It is supposed that Bristly Poppy was introduced to Madeira by men and assumed that it is the cardinal form of Opium Poppy/White Poppy (Papaver somniferum). This species is only known in cultivation and was used in ancient times to obtain opium. Today it is still harvested and processed in some Asian countries.

DOUBLE BLADDER CAMPION
SILENE UNIFLORA

BLOOM TIME
From March to May

CHARACTERISTICS

This member of the Carnation family grows up to 25 cm (10") tall. It has narrow, sharp leaves and a woody base. It develops numerous, thin and erect inflorescences that bear white blossoms at the apex. The five petals are grown together in the lower half and thus form the calyx.

SITE:
The Double Bladder Campion grows exclusively in coastal areas and populates nearly always rocky or stony soils. You will barely find it on better soils, where other plants have already settled. Most sites will be situated below the altitude of 50 m (55 yd.). At the most it can reach up to an altitude of 150 m (165 yd.). You can frequently encounter it on the Ponta São Lourenço.

INTERESTING TO KNOW:
Except for the Double Bladder Campion, many campion species use to have quite sticky superior parts. Pests will stick to this "glue". The calyxes are often compared to the crop of a dove. Only insects with a very long proboscis (e.g. butterflies) can reach the nectar. On Madeira you can find six indigenous silene species. However, until now there do not exist any investigations on them. Common Campion (Silene vulgaris) is a similar species but spread over big parts of Europe.

Purple Viper's Bugloss
Echium plantagineum

BLOOM TIME
From March to October

CHARACTERISTICS
The very hairy plant develops an up to 60 cm (24") long flower stem. It bears about 3 cm (1,2") long flowers on short stalks. The blossoms are first shining blue but change to crimson-red later. The base of the leaf rosette reminds of ribwort. The leaves are longish-ovate.

SITE:
The Purple Viper's Bugloss often grows along roadsides and on wasteland. You may find larger populations in coastal areas, mostly in the south of the island, e.g. in the hotel districts of Funchal and Caniço or on the peninsula São Lourenço. You can also encounter it in the mountains, e.g. at the Boca da Corrida where it is covering whole meadows.

INTERESTING TO KNOW:
The genus denomination refers to the shape of the bloom. The protruding stamens are supposed to resemble a snake's tongue. It also grows in the Mediterranean region. There you find more than 30 herbaceous Echium species. Purple Viper's Bugloss is the only one that managed to populate Madeira. Anyway you will encounter some shrubby species (cf. p. 65 & p. 159) as well. The Blue Viper's Bugloss is the only species that grows in Western and Central Europe. It is similar to the Purple Viper's Bugloss.

MADEIRA SEA STOCK,
MADEIRA GILLYFLOWER
MATTHIOLA MADERENSIS

BLOOM TIME
From March to August

CHARACTERISTICS
The leaves are very hairy and form a rosette from which sprouts a 50 cm (20") long flower stem. At the apex they bear several strongly purple flowers (rarely white ones) that scent sweetish, mostly at night. Like within all cruciferous species (Brassicaceae), the four petals are placed oppositely to form a cross.

SITE:
Madeira Sea Stock is mostly found in coastal areas up to an altitude of 100 m (110 yd.). Occasionally you may encounter specimens that grow on rocks in remarkably higher regions. It is a frequent plant on the peninsula São Lourenço and on the precipices at the northwest coast between São Vicente and Porto Moniz. The similar Dichromatic Wallflower (cf. p. 139) mainly appears in the laurel forest but may also reach down to the coast.

INTERESTING TO KNOW:
Madeira Sea Stock is endemic but related to those Sea Stock species that grow in the Mediterranean region and are popular ornamental plants in Western and Central Europe . It often grows in clefts where the ground consists of loose, volcanic tuff. These soils hardly oppose erosion and are thus avoided by persistent plants. Madeira Sea Stock is not affected by these problems: as a biennial, it easily changes sites.

MANDON'S CANARY MARGUERITE, PULPY CANARY MARGUERITE
ARGYRANTHEMUM PINNATIFIDUM

BLOOM TIME
Only in March and April

CHARACTERISTICS
This shrubby, woody compound flower reaches 20-50 cm (8-20") in height. Numerous, tiny, yellow blossoms are placed in the centre of the inflorescence. They are surrounded by a wreath of longish, white ligulate florets. The leaves are 5 cm (2") long, 2 cm (0,8") broad and succulent.

SITE:
In spite of the genus denomination, Mandon's Canary Marguerite is endemic to Madeira. It grows at rocky, arid, coastal sites up to an altitude of 100 m (110 yd.). It is to be encountered quite easily on the peninsula São Lourenço and on the precipices at the northwest coast between São Vicente and Porto Moniz.

INTERESTING TO KNOW:
In former times, Mandon's Canary Marguerite was assigned to the genus Chrysantheme that is widespread in the Mediterranean region. Nowadays the Canary Marguerites form a proper genus that is restricted to the Atlantic Islands. They are characterized by a shrubby, often global growth. 20 of the 24 species of this genus are growing on the Canary Islands, three on Madeira and one on the Selvagen Islands. In Europe, several of the Canary species are popular as ornamental plants for their long flowers.

BLUE BIRD'S FOOT TREFOIL
LOTUS GLAUCUS

BLOOM TIME

From March to June

CHARACTERISTICS

The low growing plant (10-30 cm/ 4-12") has a woody base and grows more in width than in height. The blue to green leaves are only a few millimetres long, hairy and slightly fleshy. The blossoms are orange-yellow. The five petals of this member of the Pea family splits up in a banner, wings and keels.

SITE:

Blue Bird's Foot Trefoil mostly grows at rocky sites in coastal regions up to an altitude of 100 m (110 yd.). Although not too frequent, it is a typical plant in these areas. Hikers can encounter it at the Ponta São Lourenço.

INTERESTING TO KNOW:

Besides Madeira, the Blue Bird's Foot Trefoil grows on all Canary Islands. Here and there it is the most frequent lotus representative of all occurring species. The denomination Bird's Foot Trefoil refers to the five petals of the flower and the three equal parts of the leaves. The botanical name lotus easily causes confusion because it reminds of the lotus flowers that were of high importance as a symbol of the Gods in ancient Egypt and India. Anyway, the latter ones are water lilies.

DESFONTAINES BEANCAPER
ZYGOPHYLLUM FONTANESII

BLOOM TIME
From January to April

CHARACTERISTICS
The about 0,5 m (1,6') tall shrub has fleshy, succulent (water storing) twigs. They are covered abundantly with leaves that are thickened to pea to egg shaped knots. They are grey to green and turn yellowish under continuous exposure to dryness. The white to pink flowers are inconspicuous.

SITE:
Desfontaines Beancaper grows at arid, rocky sites in coastal areas. It tolerates higher proportions of salt that are blown up from the sea spray. All known sites of Desfontaines Beancaper specimens are situated on the peninsula São Lourenço.

INTERESTING TO KNOW:
Until now the Desfontaines Beancaper is not described in literature for Madeira. Obviously it has gone unnoticed so far. It is widespread in Morocco and on the Canary Islands. The seed capsules can survive swimming on salted water. If they are driven to dry land they are able to germinate there. Most species of the Creosote-bush family are indigenous to the tropical outlines. Only a few and thus interesting species managed to reach the Central Atlantic and the Mediterranean regions.

COMMON ICEPLANT,
CRYSTALLINE ICEPLANT
MESEMBRYANTHEMUM CRYSTALLINUM

BLOOM TIME
From April to June

CHARACTERISTICS
The plant only grows 10-20 cm (4-8") tall. The flowers consist of numerous white to pink coloured, very thin petals and a yellow centre. The short, fleshy leaves seem to be covered with ice crystals. In fact these false crystals are storage warts that contain an aqueous liquid.

SITE:
The Common Iceplant grows up to an altitude of 200 m (220 yd.) at arid sites with sandy to rocky soils. It is especially frequent on the peninsula São Lourenço. The plant tolerates a high salt concentration both in the air and in the ground and is thus able to thrive in the immediate vicinity of the sea. Sometimes it shares its sites with the Slenderleaf Iceplant (Mesembryanthemum nodiflorum), a related species with sausage-shaped leaves.

INTERESTING TO KNOW:
The Common Iceplant is also native to the Mediterranean region and the Canary Islands, mostly to Lanzarote and Fuerteventura. In former times it was cultivated as useful plant. The plant was burnt in furnaces. Soda (sodium carbonate) could then be extracted from the ashes. It was indispensable for the production of soap. However, since the end of the 19th century it has been possible to produce soda artificially.

COASTAL AREAS

SPINELESS CENTURY PLANT
AGAVE ATTENUATA

BLOOM TIME
From December to February

CHARACTERISTICS

The big, fleshy leaves are tapered and - in contrast to other Agaves - spineless. They form an imposing rosette (Ø1m/3,3") that develops the up to 3 m (10') long flower stalk. The latter lacks branches and is curved like the neck of a swan. The numerous blooms are yellow-grey.

SITE:
The Spineless Century Plant is often grown as an ornamental plant along roadsides or on embankments. Occasionally it goes wild on fallow land. It thrives from coastal levels upwards to an altitude of 500 m (550 yd.), mostly in the drier south of the island. A large population is to be found on the embankment between the runway of the airport and the adjoining motorway.

INTERESTING TO KNOW:
The Spineless Century Plant is native to Mexico, the centre of development of all Agave species. Agaves bloom the first and only time at an age of eight to ten years and die right afterwards. The story of hundred years old agaves blooming for the first time is nothing but fairytale. Already in the 16th century, another species, the American Century Plant/Maguey (Agave americana), was introduced to the drier, warmer regions of Europe for its decorating qualities. The latter is more likely to go wild.

82

ALOE VERA, BARBADOS ALOE
ALOE BARBADENSIS

BLOOM TIME
From December to June

CHARACTERISTICS
The long, fleshy leaves of Aloe Vera form a basal rosette. They are about 30 cm (12") long and visibly tapered. The leaf margin is serrated. The flower stem is up to 80 cm (32") long and branches once or twice. It bears long inflorescences with yellow, tubular single blossoms.

SITE:
In the drier coastal areas in the south of the island you will often find the Barbados Aloe growing wild on fallow land at altitudes up to 300 m (330 yd.). Sometimes you may also encounter it in gardens and along roadsides.

INTERESTING TO KNOW:
Aloe Vera is native to the southern Mediterranean region but was already introduced to Madeira centuries ago. Its bitter sap has always been used by popular medicine to treat fever, cramps and indispositions of the immune system. The gel that is made out of the pulp was used to cure wounds, sunburns and insect stings. It is said that Aloe Vera contains an entire pharmacy. Today the positive features of this plant are being rediscovered. Already for a period of several years Aloe Vera has been included in many natural medicines, cosmetics and food. A little factory in Caniçal is specialized on Aloe Vera products.

MADEIRA SQUILL
SCILLA MADERENSIS

BLOOM TIME
Only in November and December

CHARACTERISTICS
The Liliaceous plant is usually 20-35 cm (8-14") tall but occasionally reaches up to 50 cm (20"). The quite short, broad leaves are shed off in summer. The blue, star-shaped blossoms are small (Ø 10-12 mm/0,4-0,48") and placed numerously (up to 100) on long, erect, cone-like racemes. They do not scent.

SITE:
The Madeira Squill thrives at altitudes up to 500 m (550 yd.). It prefers stony or rocky grounds in coastal areas that lack more or less any other kind of plants. It can also be found at slopes at average altitudes (up to 1000 m/1100 yd.). The rare sites of this plant use to be practically inaccessible. The interested layman will thus only encounter it in the Botanical Garden of Funchal where the Madeira Squill is cultivated in larger numbers. It is also planted in other gardens.

INTERESTING TO KNOW:
This attractive plant is endemic to Madeira, Porto Santo and the Ilhas Desertas. It also grows on the Selvagen Islands, a group of islands that are part of Madeiran administration but located further southwards, close to the Canary Islands. They are under severe protection and can only be entered with a special authorization.

ORANGE WALL LICHEN
XANTHORIA PARIETINA

BLOOM TIME
None

CHARACTERISTICS

The Orange Wall Lichen is a crustose lichen. This means that it develops a broad, leaf-shaped thallus (vegetative tissue). It is well rounded, lobed at the margins and 5-10 cm (2-4") in diameter. It is firmly joined to the rock. The fruiting bodies are situated in the centre.

SITE:
On Madeira, the Orange Wall Lichen mainly grows on rocks in coastal areas where further vegetation is sparse. It is especially frequent on the peninsula São Lourenço. It is very flexible concerning climatic conditions and thus able to find suitable sites in all parts of the island.

INTERESTING TO KNOW:
Lichens are able to survive on bare rocks and thus among the first plants to populate them. On Madeira you find these conditions at the steep coasts that are constantly exposed to erosion. Lichens support the decomposition of rock and hence collaborate on soil development. The Orange Wall Lichen is a cosmopolitan plant and also grows all over Europe (however mainly on trees). On Madeira it often occurs together with the grey, also encrusted Vesuvius Snow Lichen (Stereocaulon vesubianum). The latter is the most important pioneering plant worldwide.

ALONG THE LEVADAS

In the south of the island the average altitudes of 300-800 m (330-875 yd.) are extensively used by human beings. In the north you find the same situation - but to a smaller amount – at altitudes of 100-600 m (110-655 yd.). This zone is still located below the cloud belt that is caused by the trade winds. This belt often forms dense fogs and covers the mountains at higher altitudes. However, there is sufficient rainfall to cultivate wine, grain, potatoes and vegetables without artificial watering. Thus already the first settlers began to construct terraces that are supported by stone walls and cultivate this area. This process has been continued until recently. The formerly indigenous forest with Wax Myrtles and Madeira Green-flowered Heathers was thus largely destroyed on the mountain ridges and slopes. It survived only in restricted areas, especially in the western part of the island. The land at these altitudes is intensively used for agricultural purposes until today. Anyway, more and more hardly accessible or too small terraces have become fallow land. Irrigation channels (levadas) do often cross these zones, passing long distances without considerable gradients until their water is conducted to plantations in the coastal areas. Small tracks that meander along the levadas over a distance that amounts to a total of over 2000 km (1250 miles) have often become popular trails. The visitor can most easily experience the vegetation at average altitudes through levada walks. Only a few of the wild growing plants that are to be seen beside the cultivated plants are endemic to Madeira and were already part of the sparse undergrowth in the dry heather forest. Agricultural parcels, tracks and levadas are currently lined by "weeds" that have been accidentally introduced with seeds or by garden plants that have gone wild. This mixture has produced a hotchpotch of numerous, interesting species. The governmental department in charge cultivates systematically ornamental plants like agapanthus or hydrangeas along the levadas that are frequently used by hikers. The plants do also serve to support the tracks. Farming is not possible at upper altitudes for the high fog frequency. There you can encounter trees that are called "exotic" by the local population, such as eucalyptus, pines and acacias along the levadas. In the south they form extensive forests up to the mountainous regions. A unique landscape is to be found in the narrow, humid ravines where raging water masses use to run down after winter rainfalls. These sites were not cultivated by men and often preserved the natural vegetation – a warmth preferring form of laurel forest (cf. p. 117).

BLUE GUM TREE
EUCALYPTUS GLOBULUS

BLOOM TIME
From October to March

CHARACTERISTICS

The tree is up to 30 m (34 yd.) tall. The bark uses to peal off in stripes. Young leaves are broad, bluish and stalkless. Elder specimens have narrow, sickle-shaped leaves with stalks. The flowers consist of numerous slender, yellowish stamens. The firm seed capsules resemble buttons.

SITE:

At the southern slope of the island between Santo da Serra and Ponta do Pargo you will find a proper Blue Gum Tree belt at altitudes between 500-1000 m (550-1100 yd.). Although you may also find larger populations it occurs not that frequent in the north of Madeira.

INTERESTING TO KNOW:

The Blue Gum Tree is native to Australia. In the 1930ies it was used on Madeira to afforest areas that had formerly been pastureland on a grand scale. The project aimed at curbing erosion. The plant requires a lot of water while growing. Anyway, this demand is no problem for Madeiran site conditions. The tender wood is exported by ship to the mainland where it is processed by the paper industry. The leaves contain about 3,5% ethereal oils. The green sweets that are sold everywhere on Madeira are perfumed with these oils.

BLACK WATTLE
ACACIA MEARNSII

BLOOM TIME
All year round, peak blooming in March and April

CHARACTERISTICS
This evergreen tree is up to 10 m (11 yd.) tall and has bipinnate leaves that resemble those of the related Mimosa. However, the former ones are harder and do not fold together when touching them. The pale yellow, spherical inflorescences consist of numerous tiny, fragrant blossoms.

SITE:
You will frequently find Black Wattle on the southern half of the island at altitudes of 300-1200 m (330-1320 yd.). If you go by car you will encounter it along the road from Monte to Terreiro da Luta. Hikers will often see it along levadas at average altitudes. The Levada do Caniçal, close to Machico, seems to be a proper "Wattle-Levada".

INTERESTING TO KNOW:
Mistakenly, Black Wattle is often called "Mimosa". However, Mimosa/Sensitive Plant (Mimosa pudica) is a delicate shrub native to Brazil. Black Wattle is indigenous to Australia. Owners of private forest parcels used to afforest with the fast-growing, undemanding Black Wattle. The tender wood is of hardly any economic value but was used as a heating fuel by many households until recently. Today, ovens and stoves are fuelled by gas.

BLACKWOOD ACACIA
ACACIA MELANOXYLON

BLOOM TIME
From January to April

CHARACTERISTICS

The tree reaches 30 m (33 yd.) in height. It reminds of a pear tree for its growth but has longish, dark green, leathery leaves. Only the very youngest leaves are slightly pinnate, similar to those of the Black Wattle (cf. p. 89). Abundant pale yellow, globular blossoms are placed on panicles.

SITE:

You will find Blackwood Acacia at altitudes of 300-1000 m (330-1100 yd.) at humid sites that correspond to the natural habitat of the laurel forest. It uses to grow not too far away from settlements. You can often encounter it in the north of the island, e.g. along the Levada do Caldeirão Verde between Queimadas and Pico das Pedras.

INTERESTING TO KNOW:

In contrast to the Black Wattle, Blackwood Acacia does not have pinnate leaves. Thus you will not mix it up with Mimosa plants. These two Acacia species were both introduced from Australia and yield good furniture timber. Moreover they are supposed to put a stop to erosion. The leaves of mature specimens of Blackwood Acacia are no more than widened leaf stalks (phyllodes). This degeneration reduces the loss of water by evaporation that is of a remarkably greater amount in the case of young plants with pinnate leaves.

AUSTRALIAN CHEESEWOOD
PITTOSPORUM UNDULATUM

BLOOM TIME

From January to March; fruit bearing starts in late summer

CHARACTERISTICS

The up to 8 m (9 yd.) tall tree is easily mixed up with indigenous laurel species for its similar growth and foliage. The about 10 cm (4") long leaves have conspicuously crinkled margins. The flowers are white to yellow. The orange-red fruits contain the seeds that are embedded in a sticky liquid.

SITE:

You find the plant up to an altitude of 700 m (765 yd.) along the borders of acacia and eucalyptus forests. For example it grows quite frequently along the Levada da Serra, near to Camacha, or along the Levada dos Tornos, east of Monte. It is also to be found in several parks.

INTERESTING TO KNOW:

The tree is native to Southeast Australia. It was introduced to Madeira long ago. It is grown as an ornamental plant and as a hedge plant to protect orchards against wind. On the Azores it tends very much to go wild and thus suppresses indigenous plants. Until now it seems as if it does not cause any problems on Madeira. Anyway there is the risk of breeding with the rare Madeira Cheesewood (Pittosporum coriaceum), which would mean to distort this species. You will only encounter the latter one in gardens (Botanical Garden, Jardim Tropical Monte Palace, Ribeiro Frio). It has oval, non-undulate leaves.

BIG LEAF HYDRANGEA
HYDRANGEA MACROPHYLLA

BLOOM TIME
From June to September

CHARACTERISTICS

The dense shrub is 1-1,5 m (3,3-5') tall and has numerous firm, oval, slightly pointed leaves. The hemispherical flower umbels peep out from between the leaves. On Madeira, they use to be light blue to white for the high aluminium concentration of the soils. Otherwise the blooms would be pink.

SITE:

The Big Leaf Hydrangea requires a relatively high humidity and grows along roadsides and levadas at average altitudes (700-1400 m/765-1530 yd., even lower at the north coast). Among others, the Levada da Serra between Quatro Estradas and Portela is a proper "Hydrangea-Levada".

INTERESTING TO KNOW:

The wild form is also grown on Madeira. Its plate-shaped inflorescences consist of two types of flowers. The fertile blooms are small and inconspicuous. Placed in the centre they are surrounded by a wreath of infertile, conspicuous blooms. Already centuries ago Japanese succeeded in cultivating this colourful "exhibition flower". However, these cultivars are not able to produce seeds. Seedlings realize propagation. The French natural scientist Commerson named the genus after his girlfriend, Hortense Barré. In the 18th century he was the first to bring dried hydrangeas to Europe.

GARLEAF NIGHTSHADE
SOLANUM MAURITIANUM

BLOOM TIME
From February to October

CHARACTERISTICS
The shrub reaches up to 4 m (4,4 yd.) in height. It resembles a large potato plant and is a member of the Potato family. The big, elliptical leaves are hairy. The flower umbels consist of 10-20 purple single blossoms. Small, yellow fruits develop from the blooms.

SITE:
Garleaf Nightshade thrives at humid sites at altitudes of about 500 m (550 yd.). At the southern slope of the island it grows at the bottom of narrow valleys, in the rainy north it also lines roadsides. You will often find several specimens growing closely together. Hikers will encounter the plant e.g. at the Levada dos Tornos, close to Camacha and Monte. It also often borders eucalyptus forests above Santana and São Jorge.

INTERESTING TO KNOW:
The plant is native to Central America. At the end of the 19th century it was introduced to Madeira as an ornamental plant. Since then it has gone wild with increasing tendency. It often grows not too far away from settlements. Similar to all species of the Potato family, the plant contains solanine, a toxic glycoalkaloid, in all its parts. Intoxications are manifested by sore throats, headaches, fever and cramps. You ought not try the fruits under no circumstances.

COMMON GORSE
ULEX EUROPAEUS

CHARACTERISTICS

The spiny, very ramified shrub grows up to 2 m (6,6') tall and has firm, erectly growing twigs that stick out in all directions from the branches. Numerous leaves are placed on the twigs. They are often receded to short spines. The broom-like pea flowers are shining yellow.

SITE:
You will find Common Gorse growing on cleared surfaces in laurel forests at altitudes of 600-1400 m (655-1530 yd.): on pasturelands or along levadas that lead through eucalyptus or pine forests. It prefers sunny sites. It is frequently encountered at the border of the plateau Paúl da Serra (e.g. along the Levada do Paúl), above Camacha along the road that leads to the Poiso-Pass, along the road from Portela towards the Levada do Furado and beneath the Pico Grande.

INTERESTING TO KNOW:
The plant is indigenous to the West European heath regions. Together with the Scotch Broom (Cytisus scoparius), native to Southern Europe, it was introduced to Madeira as a forage plant. It spreads rapidly and often forms dense populations. The twigs are used to fuel ovens by the local residents. It is said that bread is especially tasty when it has been baked above gorse-fire (pão de lenha).

CAPE IVY
DELAIREA ODORATA

CHARACTERISTICS

This climber develops up to 6 m (6,5 yd.) long tendrils and thus creeps up shrubs and trees. The little, strong yellow compound flowers are organized in large umbels. The five-lobed leaves resemble those of the Common Ivy and scarcely attract attention outside bloom time.

SITE:
From coastal levels up to an altitude of 700 m (765 yd.) you will often find the Cape Ivy having gone wild on cultivated land. Hikers will easily encounter it along several levadas, for example along the Levada do Caniçal around Machico or along the Levada dos Tornos close to Camacha. It also populates rocky slopes and various gardens.

INTERESTING TO KNOW:
The Cape Ivy - formerly known as German Ivy (Senecio mikanioides) is native to South Africa. For its attractive blossoms it was introduced to Madeira. In California Cape Ivy is highly invasive and extremely difficult to control. On Madeira it does not seem to be problematical. Several representatives of this genus are even to be found in Central Europe. Anyway, these species are no climber plants. Cape Ivy is not closer related neither to the Common Ivy (Hedera helix) nor to the endemic Madeira Ivy (Hedera maderensis). The latter has heart-shaped leaves.

COMMON MORNING GLORY
IPOMOEA PURPUREA

BLOOM TIME
From September to May

CHARACTERISTICS

The Common Morning Glory resembles those related species of the Bindweed family that are growing in Europe. The five petals are strong purple with a darker vertical stripe in the middle of each. They are grown together and form a funnel. The firm leaves are heart-shaped.

SITE:

Common Morning Glory is a climber and creeps up rock faces, walls, pylons and trees. It was already introduced as an ornamental plant from South America to Europe in the 17th century. On Madeira it often goes wild today. It grows along roadsides and levadas close to settlements. It also neatly covers rubbish and compost heaps. You can encounter it at altitudes up to 500 m (550 yd.), mostly in the south.

INTERESTING TO KNOW:

The Sweet Potato (Ipomoea batatas), also native to America, is a close relative of the Common Morning Glory. Its blossoms are white on the outside and strong pink on the inside. Sweet Potato is cultivated on Madeira and yields sweet, starch containing tubers. Several species of the related European Bindweed genus Convolvulus are part of Madeira's natural flora, for example the endemic Madeira Bindweed with its white blossoms and pink stripes.

GARDEN NASTURTIUM, INDIAN CRESS
TROPAEOLUM MAJUS

BLOOM TIME
From February to September

CHARACTERISTICS

The plant develops tendrils that can either cover the ground like a carpet or creep up other plants up to 3 m (10') high. The leaves are shield-like with five or ten sketched corners. The bell-shaped blossoms consist of five petals. Their colour ranges from golden yellow to orange red.

SITE:

The Garden Nasturtium requires much sunlight and soils that are rich in nutrients. It is indigenous to the Andes, especially to Peru. It was introduced to Madeira as an ornamental plant and has often gone wild since then. It mostly grows in cultivated land at the border of agricultural parcels and levadas. You can find it up to an altitude of 800 m (875 yd.). However, it never surpasses the forest line. It is very frequent along the Levada da Serra around Camacha and along the Levada do Norte.

INTERESTING TO KNOW:

The leaves contain mustard oil glycoside and have antibiotic effects. The taste is slightly hot and reminds of watercress. Both leaves and blossoms can be used to prepare salads. Pickled in vinegar, the young buds taste similar to capers. However, on Madeira it is not common to eat them neither this nor that way.

97

West Indian Lantana, Hedgeflower
Lantana camara

BLOOM TIME
All year round, mostly in summer

CHARACTERISTICS
The 1,5 m (5′) tall shrub has square, slightly thorny twigs. The ovate leaves have a hairy bottom. The inflorescences are up to 3 cm (1,2″) broad and consist of about 20 single blossoms each. When maturing, the colour of the blooms changes from yellow to orange or from pink to purple.

SITE:
You can find the West Indian Lantana as an ornamental plant in gardens and parks, mostly at altitudes of 300-600 m (330-665 yd.), below the laurel forest zone. It has also been cultivated along roads and levadas where it tends to go wild. You will encounter it for example along the Levada dos Tornos, along the Levada da Serra (in the southeast of Madeira) or in the Palheiro Gardens.

INTERESTING TO KNOW:
The plant is native to regions from the south of the U.S.A. to South America. It was already introduced to Europe as an ornamental plant in the 17th century. The plants that are cultivated on Madeira do obviously not belong to the American wild form but are cross-breedings of various hybrids. The leaves are toxic and thus scorned by nearly all animals. Anyway, its blossoms do attract butterflies. Birds like to eat the fruits.

MONTPELLIER ROCKROSE
CISTUS MONSPELIENSIS

BLOOM TIME
From April to July

CHARACTERISTICS
The dense, up to 1 m (3,3') tall shrub has numerous, sticky leaves. They are curled up at the margin; at the bottom they feel like felt. In midsummer they turn brown. The blossoms resemble those of the Wild Rose but are smaller and white. Both leaves and blooms scent aromatically.

SITE:
The Montpellier Rockrose prefers sunny sites at the southern slope of the island at altitudes of 500-800 m (550-875 yd.). In these areas it occurs along roadsides and levadas, in pine forests and in sparse bushes. It rapidly settles on expanses that were affected by bush fires and forms larger population on there. You can encounter it for example in the region of Jardim da Serra or along the Levada do Norte between Boa Morte and Câmara de Lobos.

INTERESTING TO KNOW:
Probably the plant was once a permanent part of a dry form of laurel forest on the mountain ridges in the south of the island. It is also spread on the Canary Islands and in the Mediterranean region. On Madeira it is the only species of the Rockrose family, a family related to the roses. In the Mediterranean region you can find more than 50 Rockrose species.

CROFTONWEED,
STICKY SNAKEROOT
AGERATINA ADENOPHORA

BLOOM TIME
From March to September

CHARACTERISTICS

The 0,5-1 m (1,7-3,3') tall, herbaceous plant uses to form larger populations. The small, white, compound flowers are placed in loose umbels upon reddish stalks. The light green leaves remind of arrowheads and have serrated margins. The related Creeping Croftonweed has pale purple leaves.

SITE:
Croftonweed requires humid conditions and grows at altitudes up to 1200 m (1310 yd.). It often thrives along sheltered levadas from whereon it spreads in the adjoining forests. It also invades the laurel forest. The Portuguese name already refers to its abundant occurrence on Madeira (Abundância: abundance).

INTERESTING TO KNOW:
The plant is native to Central America and was introduced to Madeira in the middle of the 19th century. Today, Croftonweed is one of the most frequent foreign species on Madeira. This term describes plants that were introduced by men and have gone wild afterwards. Today you can find about 800 indigenous vascular plants (flowering plants and lichens) on Madeira. In contrast, there are about 550 species that have been introduced and then gone wild. They partly suppress the indigenous species and thus have a negative long-term influence on the ecosystem.

BLUE THROATWORT
TRACHELIUM CAERULEUM

BLOOM TIME
From April to August

CHARACTERISTICS
Blue Throatwort is up to 1 m (3,3') tall and of a bushy growth. It has a woody base. The large, blue-purple inflorescences resemble umbels. They are made up by small single blooms from which are protruding long styles. The leaves are pointed, slightly serrated and have tender hairs.

SITE:
Blue Throatwort grows up to an altitude of 500 m (547 yd.) above sea level. It prefers sheltered, humid sites, mostly in the valleys in the south of Madeira. It often grows on rock faces. You should look for Blue Throatwort in those areas where levadas cross steep valleys, for example the Levada Nova between Ponta do Sol and Calheta. It can also be encountered on walls. For its attractive inflorescences it is often cultivated in gardens.

INTERESTING TO KNOW:
Blue Throatwort is native to the western Mediterranean region, Portugal and Morocco. It could be possible that men introduced it to Madeira. Anyway there are scientists who assume that it has already been part of the indigenous flora. It is related to the bellflowers but you will definitely not notice any similarity in the outer appearance of these two genera.

101

RED VALERIAN
CENTRANTHUS RUBER

BLOOM TIME
From March to October

CHARACTERISTICS

The up to 50 cm (20") tall Red Valerian has small, pink to red flowers that each have a sharp spur. Numerous single blooms form umbel-like inflorescences. There exists a white-flowering form. The grey-green, partly fleshy leaves are situated opposite to each other. They are ovate.

SITE:

Up to an altitude of 600 m (655 yd.) you can find Red Valerian at sunny sites in the south of the island. It grows along roadsides and levadas, on walls and at rocky sites. It is especially frequent in the southwest near to Prazeres and Estreito da Calheta. Single specimens are to be found along the road that leads from Funchal to Curral das Freiras and in the region of Gaula.

INTERESTING TO KNOW:

The Portuguese name of Red Valerian is Rosa da Rocha (rock rose). Anyway, it is not related to roses but a member of the Valerian family. Probably it was introduced as an ornamental plant from the Mediterranean region and went wild afterwards- this is controversially discussed. The related, only rarely occurring Annual Valerian (Centranthus calcitrapae) is in any case an endemic species. The latter has pale pink flowers. It is smaller and populates rocky sites and fallow land.

LATIN AMERICAN FLEABANE,
MEXICAN DAISY
ERIGERON KARVINSKIANUS

BLOOM TIME
From March to September

CHARACTERISTICS
The blossoms resemble daisies and are the most conspicuous part of the plant. The wreath of narrow ligulate florets is white or pink; the centre of the flower is yellow. Numerous blooms on thin stalks shoot from the cushion plant. The leaves are small, narrow and pointed.

SITE:
You will most often find the Latin American Flebane on walls and rocks in cultivated land: along levadas, roadsides and rock verges. It is quite frequent everywhere up to an altitude of 1000 m (1100 yd.) and only avoids extremely arid sites. It could not succeed at sites with intact natural vegetation.

INTERESTING TO KNOW:
The Latin American Fleabane was introduced as an ornamental plant from Mexico to Madeira in ancient times. The common name refers to the assumption that the dried plants would keep away fleas. Latin American Fleabane is also cultivated as a mosquito repellent. The seeds are normally spread by wind. However, the plant can also propagate vegetatively.

PITCH TREFOIL,
ARABIAN PEA
BITUMINARIA BITUMINOSA

BLOOM TIME
From April to August

CHARACTERISTICS

The plant is 20 cm-1 m (8"-3,3') tall. The leaves are threefold. Both the leaves and the blossoms are placed upon long stalks. The blooms are typical global trefoil blooms and of a faded purple colour. Crumbling leaves and stalks produce a striking smell of asphalt.

SITE:

The Pitch Trefoil follows human settlements. It grows along various levadas and at the border of agricultural parcels. In coastal areas it is to be found both on wallow land and in natural or nature-resembling plant formations.

INTERESTING TO KNOW:

This species is also indigenous to the Canary Islands and the Mediterranean region. In ancient Greece it was used to treat snakebites. On Madeira it is commonly employed as a hair-restorer by popular medicine. Moreover it yielded a natural dye that was used for fabrics. The smell of asphalt comes from the blackish glands that cover the entire plant. This stench protects the plant against natural enemies. Thus on Madeira it is cultivated specifically around agricultural parcels to keep away rabbits and goats.

BERMUDA BUTTERCUP, AFRICAN WOODSORREL
OXALIS PES-CAPRAE

BLOOM TIME
From December to April

CHARACTERISTICS

The Bermuda Buttercup has the typical "cloverleaf". The numerous leaves form flat cushions from which develop up to 30 cm (12") tall inflorescences. They consist of several, funnel-shaped, bright yellow blooms that resemble the primroses (cowslips) that are growing wild in Europe.

SITE:
You will mostly find the Bermuda Buttercup at altitudes of 400-700 m (440-765 yd.) in areas that are intensively used for agricultural purposes. It grows along roadsides and levadas, around agricultural parcels and on abandoned cultivated land. It also occurs down to coastal levels and even on the dry peninsula São Lourenço. It is a frequent plant and uses to found larger populations. You may sometimes find cultivars with stuffed flowers as ornamental plants.

INTERESTING TO KNOW:
The plant is native to South Africa but meanwhile has become a permanent part of the wild flora on Madeira. It also grows frequently on the Canary Islands and in the Mediterranean region. The capsules will not ripen outside of its natural habitat in South Africa. On Madeira the plant propagates through subterranean breeding nodules.

PURPLE WOODSORREL
OXALIS PURPUREA

BLOOM TIME
From December to April

CHARACTERISTICS
The ground-covering plant is only a few centimetres tall. The numerous leaves are shaped like cloverleaves. The plant develops conspicuously funnel-shaped blossoms that scarcely protrude from the leaf cushion. The five petals are bright scarlet; the neck of the funnel is entirely yellow.

SITE:
The Purple Woodsorrel requires sheltered, relatively humid sites at average altitudes (200-700 m/220-765 yd.). It is most often to be found on cultivated land, in gardens and parks. You can encounter it for example in areas where oaks or sweet chestnuts line levadas (e.g. Levada dos Tornos in the region of Camacha), in the Palheiro Gardens or in the park of the Quinta do Santo da Serra.

INTERESTING TO KNOW:
As the Bermuda Buttercup (cf. p. 105), the Purple Woodsorrel was also introduced to Madeira by men. Anyway, the latter species does not spread aggressively at the expense of other plants. Today it is an essential part of Madeira's wild flora. As within all species of the genus Oxalis (Woodsorrel), the plants' leaves contain oxalic acid and oxalates (sorrel salt). Thus it is toxic to some extent.

LAVENDER SCALLOPS
BRYOPHYLLUM FEDTSCHENKOI

BLOOM TIME
All year round, mostly in spring and summer

CHARACTERISTICS
The plant reaches 30-40 cm (12-16") in height and has thick, fleshy, rounded leaves. They are grey with crimson dots and have carved margins. Little groups of orange-yellow or pale red, tubular blooms are placed wreath-like around the flower stalks and hang down from them.

SITE:
Along the Levada do Caniçal, in the valley of Machico, you can find a larger population of wild growing Lavender Scallops. Besides, it is mostly to be found in gardens, at rocky, sunny sites up to an altitude of 300 m (330 yd.). There it often grows together with the related Chandelier Plant (Bryophyllum tubiflorum). The latter is larger and has longish leaves and red blossoms.

INTERESTING TO KNOW:
Especially in the case of the Chandelier Plant, propagation is partly realized by vegetative buds that are placed on the leaves. The genus Kalanchoe is closely related to the genus Leaf of Life (Bryophyllum) but lacks the breeding nodules and is thus easy to distinguish. Both genera are indigenous to Africa and especially frequently spread in Madagascar. For their bizarre appearance they are often kept by people fond of succulents.

PURPLE MILK THISTLE
GALACTITES TOMENTOSA

BLOOM TIME
From February to September

CHARACTERISTICS

The plant grows up to 60 cm (24") tall. The hardy stalks and spiny leaves are typical features of thistles. The compound blooms consist of numerous, pale purple, tubular flowers. On the inside they are short and very pale, on the outside remarkably longer and of a more intense colour.

SITE:

The widespread plant prefers sites in the drier south of the island, mostly near to the coast. At sunny sites it can even grow up to an altitude of 1000 m (1100 yd.). You will often encounter it on the peninsula São Lourenço. It also grows on fallow land close to the hotels in Caniço and in Funchal. Moreover you can find it along various levadas that cross farmland.

INTERESTING TO KNOW:

Although it looks like a true thistle, this plant does not belong to the thistles (genus Carduus). The typical thistle-like appearance is a feature that also characterizes related genera. The Purple Milk Thistle is mainly spread in the Mediterranean region but also native to the Canary Islands. Some botanists assume that it was only introduced there by men in ancient times. This could possibly hold for Madeira as well. The name refers to the purple blossoms with white dots.

Common Agapanthus,
Oriental Nile Lily
Agapanthus orientalis

Bloom time
From May to September

Characteristics
The plant has long, narrow leaves with leaf veins that are situated parallel to each other. Up to 70 cm (28") tall stalks stick out from the foliage. Hemispherical, blue or white umbels are placed upon them. The up to 100 single blossoms are made up star-like by six petals.

Site:
You will frequently find the Common Agapanthus as an ornamental plant along levadas and roadsides from coastal levels up to altitudes of more than 1000 m (1100 yd.). It is also often cultivated in gardens and parks. Public authorities use to decorate traffic islands and barriers with Common Agapanthus. The plant propagates by stolons (runners) but does not have any tendency to go wild.

Interesting to know:
The plant originates in South Africa. In its natural habitat the flower is blue. The white form is only a cultivar. Agapanthus orientalis is often mixed up with African Nile Lily (Agapanthus africanus). Anyway it has been separated from the species Agapanthus africanus. The true African Nile Lily is smaller, the umbels contain fewer flowers and the leaves often have stripes. The genus denomination is derived from the Greek words "agape" (love) and "anthos" (flower).

BELLADONNA LILY, CAPE BELLADONNA
AMARYLLIS BELLADONNA

BLOOM TIME
From September to
November

CHARACTERISTICS

The leaves develop after the flowers and dry out in summer. Then, only the bulbs do partly stick out from the ground. In autumn they shoot 30-40 cm (12-16") long inflorescences on which are placed wreaths of large funnel-like blossoms. The tips of the six petals are conspicuously pink.

SITE:
The Belladona Lily is native to South Africa. On Madeira it has often been planted along roadsides and levadas. From there on it has gone wild and entered pine and eucalyptus forests where it often is the only plant growing in the undergrowth. It is very frequent in the southwest of Madeira, at altitudes between 300 and 900 m (330-985 yd.).

INTERESTING TO KNOW:
In one of the eclogues ("Bucolica") written by the Roman poet Virgil (70-19 BC), the shepherd Tyros lauds the beauty of the girl Amaryllis on his flute. Thus was created the name of various ornamental plants. From all these species, only the Belladona Lily is assigned to the genus Amaryllis today. The remaining species that were known as Amaryllis have been classified as belonging to other genera. The plant is not related to the Deadly Nightshade that is commonly known as "Belladonna".

WATSONIA, CAPE BUGLE LILY
WATSONIA BORBONICA

BLOOM TIME
From June to August

CHARACTERISTICS
Watsonia belongs to the Iris family. It has very long, narrow leaves. The inflorescences remind of Gladioli and are coloured either white or pink. Watsonia propagates by root runners; thus you will always find several plants standing closely together and forming a dense thicket.

SITE:
Watsonia was frequently cultivated along roadsides and levadas in the more humid north of the island. It grows at altitudes of 200-700 m (220-765 yd.). You can encounter it especially often in Santana, mostly along the road that leads towards Achada do Teixeira. It does not tend to go wild.

INTERESTING TO KNOW:
Watsonia is indigenous to South Africa. On Madeira it mostly blossoms around St. John's Day (24th of July). For this fact and for its flag-shaped inflorescences it got the common English denomination "St. John's Staff". At weekends in July/August, mainly in Santana but also in other areas, you can observe women harvesting the single blooms. They are used to create flower carpets on the occasion of the Festa do Senhor (Epiphany). They will be ruined immediately by the following procession.

MONTBRETIA
CROCOSMIA CROCOSMIIFLORA

BLOOM TIME
July and August

CHARACTERISTICS

This about 50 cm (20") high member of the Iris family has long, very narrow, pointed leaves. The inflorescences are placed upon stalks. They seem to be quite filigree and consist of orange to red single blossoms. Plants usually stay together in larger groups.

SITE:

The Montbretia was often cultivated along roadsides and levadas at altitudes of 200-750 m (220-820 yd.). It also is a frequent garden plant. Montbretia does not tend to go wild. Hikers may for example encounter it above Portela along the way to the Lamaceiros forester's house and along various levadas at the southern coast.

INTERESTING TO KNOW:

The popular cultivated form of Montbretia is the product of a cross-breeding of the two South African wild species Crocosmia pottsii and Crocosmia aurea. It was cultivated 1882 in Nancy (France). Members of the Iris family are usually easy to plant. Gladioli and freesias, both popular as ornamental plants, and crocuses do also belong to the Iris family. The denomination "Montbretia" is derived from the French natural scientist A.F.E. Coquebert de Montbret.

ARUM LILY, CALLA LILY
ZANTEDESCHIA AETHIOPICA

BLOOM TIME
From November to June

CHARACTERISTICS
The plant belongs to the Arum family. It is 50-80 cm (20-32") tall and has big, arrow-shaped leaves. The leaf stalks contain a toxic, corrosive sap. An attractive, scenting flower is placed on the top of each of the strong flower stalks. The bloom consists of a single, white, funnel-shaped bract.

SITE:
Arum Lily is often to be found as an ornamental plant in gardens and parks, e.g. in the Botanical Garden or in the Palheiro Gardens. It tends to grow wild at humid sites in valley bottoms in the south of the island, at altitudes of 400-800 m (440-875 yd.). It can be encountered e.g. along the Levada do Norte or around Camacha. In the north of Madeira you will more likely find it in coastal areas.

INTERESTING TO KNOW:
Madeira is not the natural habitat of the Arum Lily. Although its botanical denomination may give rise to this supposition, it is not native to Ethiopia either but to South Africa. The plant sprouts again even from bare fragments of its rhizome. Thus it is very easy to propagate it at humid and frost-free sites. On Madeira, farmer's wives use to cultivate Arum Lily in vineyards or meadows and later sell roots and flowers on the markets.

113

THREECORNER LEEK
ALLIUM TRIQUETRUM

BLOOM TIME
From March to May

CHARACTERISTICS
The leaves develop from the base of the stalks and are very long and narrow. As within all Allium species they slightly smell of leek. The stalk has three sharp edges. The inflorescences consist of 5-15 hanging single blossoms. They do all turn to the same direction.

SITE:
The Threecorner Leek requires a certain humidity and is thus to be found most frequently along levadas. Plants use to grow in groups. Threecorner Leek prefers an altitude of about 500 m (550 yd.) in the south of the island but never surpasses the forest line. Among other sites you can encounter larger populations along the Levada do Norte between the Cabo Girão and Estreito de Câmara de Lobos.

INTERESTING TO KNOW:
The plant is spread in the whole Western Mediterranean region. Men probably introduced it to Madeira. The genus Allium contains about 100 species. Among these are onion, garlic, leek, chives and the broad-leaved garlic. The Threecorner Leek contains only a very low concentration of ethereal oils with sulphuric compounds (determining feature for the smell) and is thus not suitable as a kitchen herb.

ITALIAN GLADIOLUS
GLADIOLUS ITALICUS

BLOOM TIME
Only April and May

CHARACTERISTICS
This wild Gladiolus is about 50 cm (20") tall. The pink to red blossoms are visibly smaller than those of the popular cultivars. The flower stalks bear loose series of irregular blooms with only two symmetrical edges. All blossoms turn into the same direction. The leaves are long and sharp.

SITE:
The Italian Gladiolus follows human settlements. It thrives both along agricultural parcels and along levadas that cross cultivated land. It is also to be found along roadsides and embankments. It is very frequent in the east of the island, for example around Faial or along the Levada do Caniçal close to Machico.

INTERESTING TO KNOW:
The Italian Gladiolus is likely to grow in grain fields in the entire Mediterranean region. Thus it is possible that its seeds have been accidentally brought to Madeira with cereal seeds. It is uncertain whether the plant is part of the natural flora of Madeira and the Canary Islands or not. Besides of Europe, wild gladioli only grow in South Africa. The latter ones are the cardinal species of the popular gladiolus cultivars with their large blossoms in varying colours.

In the Laurel Forest

The laurel forest (laurissilva in Portuguese) is the epitome of a typical Madeiran vegetation form. In the south of the island the drier mountain ridges (above an altitude of 300 m/330 yd.) were populated by Madeira Green-flowered Heather, Wax Myrtle and Canary Laurel. The stands were already reduced severely by clearances in the 15th and 16th century. Anyway, the laurel forest is still widespread in the north of Madeira where it occupies an area of about 10000 ha (25000 acres). This ground corresponds to an eighth part of the island's surface. The north of the island is wetter than the south. Around noon you can observe nearly daily a cloud layer above an altitude of 500 m (550 yd.). It is due to the prevailing north winds and will usually disperse in the evening.

The laurel forest is especially sumptuous and species-rich in this foggy zone. The dominant plant is the Azorean Laurel; other occurring members of the laurel family are the Stinklaurel and the Madeira Mahogany. You will also encounter numerous smaller trees and shrubs, herbs and ferns. Most species of the laurel forest do not tolerate frost and thus do not thrive at altitudes higher than 1300 m (1420 yd.). Nightly frosts and snow are frequent winter features of the highest mountain regions on Madeira (cf. p. 155). A laurel forest variation that is more tolerant towards dryness can thrive down nearly to coastal areas in the north of the island. However, fields and settlements were constructed below the cloud layer and the forest is today restricted to some narrow ravines. Millions of years ago, similar forests also occurred in Central Europe but disappeared gradually with the climate change that was caused by the creation of the Alps and the ice ages. Today, laurel forest is restricted to Madeira, several Canary Islands and the Azores Islands.

On Madeira, the public authorities founded a natural reserve in 1982 and put the remaining stands of laurel forest under conservation. In 1992, the UNESCO assigned it to the world cultural heritage. The until recently popular usage (production of timber for construction and furniture, extraction of firewood and cattle feed, pasturing of goats) is now forbidden. Hunting the Madeira Laurel Pigeon has also been prohibited. This animal feeds on the fruits of laurel trees and hereby contributes to its distribution. Thus the forest can also recover at sites close to settlements where it was destructed in earlier days. The park of Ribeiro Frio offers a good overview of the flora (cf. p. 195). You can go hiking through well-preserved laurel forests e.g. around Ribeiro Frio, Queimadas and Rabaçal.

In the Laurel Forest

Stinklaurel, Fetid Laurel
Ocotea foetens

Bloom Time
From November to June; bears fruits in autumn

Characteristics
The up to 40 m (44 yd.) tall Stinklaurel is the most tremendous tree of laurel forest. Its leaves remind of the Azorean Laurel and usually have two, sometimes four large glands in the angles of the lowest leaf veins. These are recognized as dents from the bottom. The fruits resemble acorns.

Site:
You will find Stinklaurel in the upper zone of the laurel forest at altitudes of 1100-1500 m (1200-1640 yd.). It requires a humid soil and thus often grows in creek beds or close to sources. The largest population is to be found at the Fanal at the northern edge of the plateau Paúl da Serra. Hikers will see the tree below the southern face of the Pico Grande, on the way from the Encumeada-Pass towards the Pico Ruivo or around Fajã da Nogueira.

Interesting to know:
The Stinklaurel is endemic to Madeira and the Canary Islands. It belongs to the laurel family but is unsuitable as a spice. For unknown reasons the first settlers called it Til (linden tree). The usage of its timber for construction and production of furniture came to an end only some decades ago. The freshly felled wood smells unpleasantly but the stench evaporates rapidly. Today the tree is under conservation.

AZOREAN LAUREL
LAURUS AZORICA

BLOOM TIME
From February to April; bears fruits from May to September

CHARACTERISTICS
The Azorean Laurel can grow up to 25 m (28 yd.) tall. However, shrubby specimens with several thin trunks are more frequent. The leathery leaves are bigger than those of the popular Bay Laurel. On the bottom there are tiny glands in the angles of the leaf veins. The fruits resemble olives.

SITE:
You can find the Azorean Laurel in all zones of the laurel forest up to an altitude of 1400 m (1530 yd.). There it uses to be the most frequent tree. Beautiful populations are preserved in the north. The largest forest extends from Fajã da Nogueira over Ribeiro Frio to the area above Portela.

INTERESTING TO KNOW:
Azorean Laurel is native to the Azores, Madeira, the Canary Islands and Morocco. It is the closest relative to the Mediterranean Bay Laurel (Laurus nobilis). The leaves of the Azorean Laurel do also serve as spices but you need four times the amount of Bay Laurel to produce the same effect. After peeling off the bark, the Madeirans use to take the branches for the famous meat skewer (espetada). The fruits yield the laurel oil that was used traditionally both to light and to treat a multitude of illnesses. It is unsuitable as culinary oil.

MADEIRAN MAHOGANY
PERSEA INDICA

BLOOM TIME

From June to November;
bears fruits in late autumn

CHARACTERISTICS

The 15-25 m (16,5-28 yd.) tall
tree is one of the tallest trees
of the native flora. It has large,
up to 20 cm (8") long leaves
that are placed spirally around
the twigs. The elder leaves
turn to a shining red before
they are shed off. The flowers are inconspicuous. The
fruits resemble tiny avocados.

SITE:

You will find the Madeira Mahogany at shady
sites in the laurel forest. It is a typical tree
in its lower and warmer zones and grows at
altitudes of 500-1400 m (550-1530 yd.). It is
especially frequent on the southern half of the
island where you can encounter some remaining stands of laurel forest in humid valleys.

INTERESTING TO KNOW:

Although the Madeira Mahogany belongs to the
laurel family, it has got toxic leaves. The plant is
endemic to Madeira and the Canary Islands.
The related species Avocado (Persea americana)
is often cultivated on Madeira. It has similar,
but larger and edible fruits. The small fruits
of Madeira Mahogany are inedible for human
beings. The splendid, red-brown timber was
used for the production of furniture and exported to Great Britain in former times. It was
sold under the denomination "mahogany". The
tree has been under conservation since 1982.

CANARY LAUREL
APOLLONIAS BARBUJANA

BLOOM TIME

From February to May; bears fruits in autumn

CHARACTERISTICS

This very ramified tree reaches 10-20 m (11-22 yd.) and often grows crookedly. The long-ish, dark green, glossy leaves have curled margins. They often have spherical protuberances. The blooms are yellow-ish and inconspicuous. The fleshy fruits are olive-shaped.

SITE:

The Canary Laurel grows in the lower zones of the laurel forest and scarcely surpasses an altitude of 700 m (765 yd.). In the north it even grows in coastal areas. It thrives both in ravines and on dry slopes, even on rock faces. Hikers can encounter it for example in the nature reserve Ribeira do Tristão below Achadas da Cruz.

INTERESTING TO KNOW:

You will observe that parts of the leaves are turning out. These are gall formations that are evoked by a worm-shaped, white species of mites that has specialized in populating this tree. The excretions stimulate the leaves to their unusual growth. You can easily distinguish the Canary Laurel from other laurel species by these bumps. Canary Laurel is endemic to Madeira and the Canary Islands. The hard, red-brown timber was once exported as "Canary ebony". The leaves are unsuitable as spices.

WAX MYRTLE,
AZOREAN CANDLEBERRY TREE
MYRICA FAYA

BLOOM TIME
From March to May; bears fruit from late summer to late autumn

CHARACTERISTICS
The Wax Myrtle hardly never surpasses 5 m (5,5 yd.) in height. The narrow, lanceolate leaves are placed spirally around the erect, upright twigs. The inconspicuous catkins grow among the leaves. Female trees develop black fruits that resemble little blackberries out of these catkins.

SITE:
The Wax Myrtle is the dominant plant on relatively dry mountain ridges in the lower zones of the laurel forest (up to 1000 m/1100 yd.). In these areas it grows together with the Madeira Green-flowered Heather. At upper altitudes the Tree Heather joins the two species. Hikers can often encounter the Wax Myrtle around Rabaçal, e.g. along the Levada das 25 Fontes.

INTERESTING TO KNOW:
On Portuguese, the Wax Myrtle is called Faia (= beech). Anyway it does not resemble beeches. Besides Madeira, it is native to the Azores and the Canary Islands. At the end of the 19th century, emigrants introduced it to Hawaii where nowadays it causes many problems by spreading rapidly on expense of the native tree species. A close relative, the Bog Myrtle (Myrica gale) is even growing in the heath regions of Northwest Europe. The fruits are not very tasty but used to be eaten in times of misery.

LILY OF THE VALLEY TREE
CLETHRA ARBOREA

BLOOM TIME
From July to September

CHARACTERISTICS
The tree is relatively small (2-7 m/6,6-23'). It has upright twigs. Groups of leaves are placed spirally upon them. The leaves are glossy and have slightly serrated margins. Leaf stalks and leaf veins are of a conspicuously red colour. The blooms are white and hang on long racemes.

SITE:
The plant is quite frequent and grows in the lower zones of the laurel forest at altitudes of 400-800 m (440-875 yd.). It is often planted along roadsides, e.g. along the road from Santana to the Achada do Teixeira. You can also often encounter it in parks, e.g. in Ribeiro Frio.

INTERESTING TO KNOW:
The Lily of the Valley Tree is the only European member of the quite small Pepperbush family. This plant family was much more widespread in the so-called tertiary (paleogene, lower neogene) when it even grew in Central Europe. Even amber that was found in the Baltic Sea contained fossil leaves of the genus Clethra. Today you will only find species of this genus on Madeira, in Latin America and in Southeast Asia. On Madeira the Lily of the Valley Tree was intensively used. The flexible timber was used to produce poles; the leaves were fed to animals. Today the tree is under conservation.

HIGH PICCONIA
PICCONIA EXCELSA

BLOOM TIME
From February to July

CHARACTERISTICS

The 3-15 m (10-50') tall tree has a whitish bark. The white blooms are situated in a raceme. They become olive-shaped, blue to black berries. The leaves are broader than those of the related olive tree and situated in opposite pairs – a structure that is unique in the laurel forest.

SITE:
The High Picconia grows in the lower zones of the laurel forest at altitudes of 800-1000 m (875-1100 yd.). You will hardly find it at natural sites. It is cultivated for example around the trout farm of Ribeiro Frio and in the Jardim Tropical Monte Palace (in the section of endemic Madeiran flora).

INTERESTING TO KNOW:
Besides Madeira, the High Picconia only grows on the Canary Islands. A closely related species is endemic to the Azores. There are no species of the genus Picconia growing on the European mainland or in Britain. Both the High Picconia and the Azorean Picconia yield a precious timber that was used for the carpentry of furniture. Both species have thus become rare on the respective islands. Like all other species that grow in the laurel forest, the High Picconia is under conservation today.

MADEIRA HOLLY
ILEX PERADO MADERENSIS

BLOOM TIME
From April to May; bears fruits in autumn

CHARACTERISTICS
The low tree (2-5 m/6,6-16,5') has an erect trunk and dense branches. The ovate, leathery leaves are hardly serrated. Twigs that bear flowers often have leaves that are only prickly at the tip. The blooms are inconspicuously whitish. Female trees bear decorative red fruits. They are toxic.

SITE:
The Madeira Holly only grows in the laurel forest. It mainly occurs in its lower, warmer zones (500-1000 m/547-1100 yd.) and prefers sheltered sites below the canopy of taller laurel trees. It is quite rare in its natural habitat but often cultivated in parks, for example in the Palheiro Gardens or in Ribeiro Frio.

INTERESTING TO KNOW:
The Madeira Holly is a subspecies of the Perado Holly. Further subspecies are indigenous to the Canary Islands and the Azores. The Canary Holly (Ilex canariensis) also grows on Madeira. Its leaves are longer, obtuse at the base and hardly serrated. It is more tolerant towards drought and thus thrives also in the undergrowth of Tree Heathers. Both species are closely related to the much more prickly European Holly (Ilex aquifolium).

In the Laurel Forest

Madeira Green-flowered Heather
Erica scoparia maderincola

Bloom time
From April to June

Characteristics

As the very similar Tree Heather (cf. p. 157) it can be several metres tall and develop thick trunks. Usually it remains smaller. The blossoms are pale pink. The needle-like leaves are lighter and longer than those of the Tree Heather and stick out spirally. Young twigs are reddish.

Site:

Together with the Tree Heather, the Madeira Green-flowered Heather forms extensive forests at upper altitudes. Anyway it only scarcely populates the highest mountain areas but is to be found much more frequently on dry mountain ridges in the zone of laurel forest where it usually grows next to the Wax Myrtle (cf. p. 122).

Interesting to know:

This Heather should not be mixed up with the Scotch Heather (genus Calluna). The twigs of both species are suitable for the production of brooms. Green-flowered Heather (Erica scoparia) and Tree Heather (Erica arborea) are also spread in the macchia scrubland of the Mediterranean region but only reach shrub-like dimensions there. A third species growing on Madeira is the endemic Madeira Bell Heather (Erica maderensis). It resembles the Bog Heather (Erica tetralix) but grows exclusively in the mountains and blossoms in July/August.

Lanceolate Elder, Madeira Elder
Sambucus lanceolata

Bloom time
May and June

Characteristics

The 3-7 m (10-23') tall tree resembles the Black Elder that is spread in Central Europe. The leaves are hand-shaped and consist of seven or nine leaflets. The small, white to yellowish blossoms are grouped in umbels. Ripe fruits are coloured yellow to grey.

Site:
The Lanceolate Elder grows in shady ravines in the laurel forest. In the north it thrives down to an altitude of 300 m (330 yd.), the upper limit is at 1300 m (1420 yd.). It has become rare in its natural habitat. Hikers can encounter it in the Caldeirão Verde. Another big population is to be found in valley bottoms at the southern face of Paúl da Serra, along the Levada do Paúl.

Interesting to know:
Men introduced the Black or Common European Elder (Sambucus nigra) to Madeira. Here and there you can encounter it on cultivated land. On Madeira it usually stays visibly smaller than the Lanceolate Elder (average height of 2-3 m (6,6-10')). In former times its berries were taken for the production of juice, jam or tea. Nearly all parts of the plant were used by popular medicine. It is not known that the Lanceolate Elder was of such usage. Fruits and leaves are thought to be toxic.

MELLIFEROUS SPURGE
EUPHORBIA MELLIFERA

BLOOM TIME
From February to April

CHARACTERISTICS

The shrub is several metres tall. The blossoms are inconspicuous, dark brown and scent intensively of honey. The up to 20 cm (8") long, dark green leaves are placed on the tips of the twigs. Milky sap issues from the leaves when damaging them. As within most Spurge species, the sap is toxic.

SITE:

Melliferous Spurge grows at shady, humid sites in the laurel forest, especially in the north of the island. It is quite frequent in laurel forests.

INTERESTING TO KNOW:

The Spurge family contains more than 160 species that are spread in various climate zones. The species that are known in Western and Central Europe are herbaceous and inconspicuous. The species that grow in the Mediterranean region are smaller, ramified shrubs. The tropical species reach tree-like dimensions and often resemble cactuses. The Spurge species of the Atlantic islands do have an intermediate position concerning size and shape. On the Canary Islands you can find some cactus-like plants. On Madeira you only encounter two indigenous species, the tree-like Melliferous Spurge and the shrubby Smooth Spear-leaved Spurge (cf. p. 67). There also occur various herbaceous, non-endemic species that mainly grow in coastal areas.

Madeira Teline, Shrub Trefoil
Teline maderensis

Bloom time
June and July

Characteristics

The very ramified shrub is up to 5 m (5,5') tall. Its growth, shape and flowers resemble a broom. However, its twigs and leaves are softer and strangely grey-green. The small leaves are ovate in reverse and often organized in groups of three. Numerous yellow to orange pea flowers are placed at the tips of the twigs.

Site:
The Madeira Teline grows up to an altitude of 1200 m (1310 yd.) in the laurel forest zone. Hikers can encounter it at the descent from the Eira do Serrado to Curral das Freiras or below the Pico Grande. The smaller subspecies Teline maderensis paivae has more globular, less grey leaves and grows at rock faces in coastal areas.

Interesting to know:
Buds and leaves of Madeira Teline are likely to be eaten by the endemic Madeira Laurel Pigeon. Madeira Teline is the only species of the genus Teline that is native to Madeira. On the Canary Islands, botanists have already identified ten endemic Teline species. The Montpellier Teline is spread in the entire Mediterranean region. It has been brought to Madeira and is now growing wild. Its flower racemes are not placed at the tip of the twigs but in the leaves' angles.

ANDROGYNIC SEMELE, CLIMBING BUTCHER'S BROOM
SEMELE ANDROGYNA

BLOOM TIME
Only April and May

CHARACTERISTICS
The leaves of this climber are severely receded. Short shoots have developed to leave-like compounds. They are leathery, glossy and pointed and have short stalks. Creamy flowers that are grouped in little balls are placed upon them. Later appear red, well-rounded berries.

SITE:
The Androgynic Semele mainly grows in the lower zones of the laurel forest up to an altitude of about 800 m (875 yd.). At humid sites in the north of the island it can occasionally thrive below the laurel forest line. It creeps up to treetops like a liana. It is quite frequent along the Levada do Central around Lamaceiros, above Porto Moniz.

INTERESTING TO KNOW:
Besides Madeira, the Androgynic Semele is endemic to the Canary Islands. It is somehow the tropical element of the laurel forest on the Atlantic Islands. The tropical rainforest favours lianas that reach the treetops without a proper trunk and are thus advantaged in the battle for the vital light. Therefore it is not surprising that 90% of all climber plants are native to the Tropics.

KAHILI GINGER LILY
HEDYCHIUM GARDNERIANUM

BLOOM TIME
August and September

CHARACTERISTICS

The nodules resemble those of ginger plants. The flexible, about 1 m (3,3') long stalks bow to the ground for the weight of the 20-40 cm (8-16") long leaves. An attractive, spadix-shaped inflorescence develops on the tip of each stalk. The blooms are orange, the long stamens reddish.

SITE:
You will find the Kahili Ginger Lily nearly exclusively on the northern half of the island where it thrives up to an altitude of 650 m (710 yd.). It mostly grows along roadsides from where it penetrates into the laurel forest.

INTERESTING TO KNOW:
The Kahili Ginger Lily originates from the East Himalayas and was introduced to Madeira as an ornamental plant in the middle of the 19th century. It goes wild from parks and gardens and is today supposed to be the most aggressive foreign species in the laurel forest. It populates cleared or disturbed soils more easily than the native flora does and is thus an especially dreadful pest at these sites. The ground covering roots prevent the settlement of other plant species. The natural park administration has launched a project to control the pest: either the roots are cut up by machine or the plant is suffocated with the help of black plastic foils.

GIANT SOW THISTLE,
SHRUBBY SOW THISTLE
SONCHUS FRUTICOSUS

BLOOM TIME

From April to August; mainly in June/July

CHARACTERISTICS

The up to 3 m (10') tall shrub has evergreen, serrated leaves that can reach ·40 cm (16") in length. The blossoms are golden-yellow and up to 7 cm (2,8") in diameter. The plant belongs to the compound flowers and resembles an oversized dandelion. In fact it is related to this species.

SITE:
The Giant Sow Thistle grows mainly in the laurel forest where it populates rocky slopes and embankments with stony soils. You can also encounter it at other, humid sites.

INTERESTING TO KNOW:
In former times the Giant Sow Thistle was specifically cultivated as cattle feed at average altitudes. Sow Thistles are spread in Europe and often grows in weed populations or on meadows where they are mainly eaten by geese. On Madeira you can find six Sonchus species. Leaves and flowers contain a bitter principle that is probably more or less toxic to human beings. Anyway they serve as food for the Madeira Laurel Pigeon that is native to the laurel forest. If the plant is damaged, a great amount of a milky sap will issue. Therefore the Portuguese name is "leituga" (leite=milk).

BIG-LEAVED BUTTERCUP, BIG-LEAVED CROWFOOT
RANUNCULUS CORTUSIFOLIUS

BLOOM TIME
From April to June, at upper altitudes to July

CHARACTERISTICS
The strong perennial is up to 1 m (3,3') tall. The velvet leaves are lobed. Those developing at the stalk bases are especially imposing (Ø 15-30 cm/6-12") while those sprouting at higher spots are clearly smaller. The five-petaled, yellow, 5 cm (2") broad blooms resemble European Buttercup species.

SITE:
You will most likely find the Big-leaved Buttercup at shady, constantly wet sites in the laurel forest. It requires soils that are rich in humus and is to be found most frequently in the nature park close to Ribeiro Frio and along roadsides and levadas. It prefers altitudes of 700-1400 m (765-1530 yd.) but comes down to an altitude of 250 m (273 yd.) in the humid ravines of the north. It can also be encountered in the mountains - however it is much smaller there.

INTERESTING TO KNOW:
All members of the Buttercup family contain anemonin, a toxin that kills off septic bacteria. Thus the leaves can support high amounts of humidity without decomposing. Ranunculus cortusifolius is not the only member of the Buttercup family that grows on Madeira, but the most splendid one. It is also endemic to the Canary Islands and the Azores. It is often worth looking for other rare plants in its vicinity.

133

PINNATE CANARY MARGUERITE
ARGYRANTHEMUM PINNATIFIDUM
PINNATIFIDUM

BLOOM TIME
From April to July

CHARACTERISTICS

The up to 1,5 m (5') tall shrub has large, strongly serrated leaves. The numerous flowers can reach 10 cm (4") in diameter. Like Marguerites it has got numerous, small, yellow blooms that are placed basket-like on the inside and surrounded by a wreath of conspicuous, white ligulate florets.

SITE:

The Pinnate Canary Marguerite is a typical plant of the laurel forest. You can for example find it around Ribeiro Frio. It is often cultivated as an ornamental plant both in gardens and along roadsides and levadas. In contrast, the Mandon's Canary Marguerite (cf. p. 78) only grows in the immediate vicinity of the coast. A third sub-species, the Mountain Canary Marguerite (Agryranthemum pinnatifidum montanum), is to be found in the mountains at an altitude of about 1500 m (1640 yd.).

INTERESTING TO KNOW:

The three subspecies of Argyranthemum that have adapted to very different sites are preliminary forms of proper species. The Canary Marguerites are a good example of how various species can develop from one cardinal form. This development is a typical feature of volcanic islands that have been populated by only a few plant species after their formation.

BLACK PARSLEY
MELANOSELINUM DECIPIENS

BLOOM TIME
From April to July

CHARACTERISTICS
Several large, lobed leaves are placed on the tip of a woody trunk. They remind of parsley but are of completely different dimensions. The plant grows up to 2,5 m (10') tall. The small, white blossoms form dense umbels that resemble hogweed plants. Later black fruits develop out of the flowers.

SITE:
Wet, sheltered sites at altitudes of 500-800 m (547-875 yd.) are the natural habitat of the Black Parsley. In the north of the island it can be found in the lower zone of the laurel forest, e.g. along the way from Ribeiro Frio to the viewing point Balcões. In the south it grows at the bottom of valleys where it can reach ground water. At upper altitudes it is still cultivated as cattle feed here and there, e.g. in Jardim da Serra, São Roque do Faial, etc.

INTERESTING TO KNOW:
The plant is endemic to Madeira and the Azores. Scientists still lack detailed information about Black Parsley. It belongs to the Umbelliferous plants and is thus closely related to parsley, fennel and celery. Umbelliferous plants do all contain a quite high concentration of ethereal oils. Many of them are used as food or spice. However, Black Parsley seems to be unpalatable or even toxic for human beings.

135

Madeira Ragwort
Pericallis Aurita

Bloom Time

From May to August, mainly June/July

Characteristics

The shrubby plant is 0,5-1,2 m (1,7-4') tall. The leaves are heart-shaped, slightly lobed at the margins and felty at the underside. The inflorescences consist of many compound flowers that are purple to violet on the inside. The outer margin is made up by white to pale violet ligulate florets.

Site:

The Madeira Ragwort prefers altitudes of 600-1400 m (655-1530 yd.). You will often find it in the laurel forest in the north of the island where it grows in the trees' shadow or at rocky sites. It also grows at humid rock faces, quite frequently for example along the Levadas of Rabaçal.

Interesting to know:

The genus Ragwort is endemic to the Macaronesian Islands. It contains 14 species. 12 of them are native to the Canary Islands, only one to Madeira and the Azores respectively. All Ragwort species prefer certain humidity and originate from the laurel forests. In former times they were assigned to the groundsels (genus Senecio). On Madeira you will also find several species of this genus. Ragworts are distinguished by Senecio species for example by their purple or white but never yellow ligulate florets.

MADEIRA SORREL
RUMEX MADERENSIS

BLOOM TIME
From May to August

CHARACTERISTICS
The plant strongly resembles the European sorrel species but is larger (up to 1 m/3,3') and has a woody base. The triangular leaves remind of the tip of a lance and are conspicuously blue to green coloured. They taste slightly sour. Both the stalks and the sparse flower panicles are reddish.

SITE:
Madeira Sorrel mostly grows in the laurel forest zone up to an altitude of 1200 m (1310 yd.) but is even to be found down to an altitude of only 200 m (220 yd.). It prefers certain humidity and is often planted along roadsides and levadas. It also grows at swampy sites where the forest has been cleared, for example at the rock face of the Pico Grande. The plant is conspicuous and thus easy to find.

INTERESTING TO KNOW:
Madeira Sorrel is endemic to Madeira and the Canary Islands. You can find several other species of the genus Rumex on Madeira. They partly belong to the native flora, partly have been brought to the island and are all smaller and more rare than Madeira Sorrel. All Rumex species contain a mixture of sorrel salt and oxalic acid. In large amounts this substance is toxic both for animals and for human beings.

LARGE-LEAVED SAINT JOHN'S WORT
HYPERICUM GRANDIFOLIUM

BLOOM TIME

All year round, mainly from
March to August

CHARACTERISTICS

The evergreen shrub is 0,5-1,5
m (1,8-5') tall. As within most
Hypericum species the leaves
are opposite, 4-9 cm (1,6-3,6")
long and lengthened-ovate.
The flowers are quite big (Ø
4 cm/1,6"). Young shoots and
leaves are often conspicuously red-brown. On Madeira
there are eight species.

SITE:

The Large-leaved Saint John's Wort grows at
humid, shady sites from the upper coastal zone
(from 300 m/330 yd.) up to the laurel forest area.

INTERESTING TO KNOW:

Saint John's Wort is called "malfadura" in Portuguese. This means "wards off the evil". The
botanical denomination comes from Greek and
has a similar significance: "hypereikona" means
"against spook". In Europe, the plant has been
supposed to have magic powers for centuries.
On St. John's Day (24th of June), flowering
twigs are put behind windows and doors to
prevent evil spirits. Some species issue a red
sap when crumbling their blooms. In heathen
days this sap was supposed to be the blood of
the sun-god who sacrificed himself to the female deity on the date of summer solstice. The
Christians passed this symbolism on John the
Baptist. The colour is produced by the crystal-
line hypericin that is contained in the flowers.

DICHROMATIC WALLFLOWER, MADEIRA MOUNTAIN STOCK ERYSIMUM BICOLOR

BLOOM TIME

From November, mainly from March to May

CHARACTERISTICS

The shrub reaches about 1 m (3,3') in height and has narrow, evergreen leaves with slightly serrated margins. Each four petals are placed cross-shaped towards each other. Young blooms are white to yellowish but turn pink to purple later. Just before they wilt they change to white once again.

SITE:

The Dichromatic Wallflower is the most frequent of all conspicuously flowering plants in the laurel forest. You find it at many shady spots along the levadas of the laurel forest areas. It naturally populates rocky sites. You can observe it from the coast up to high mountain regions.

INTERESTING TO KNOW:

The Dichromatic Wallflower also grows on the Canary Islands. Outside the Macaronesian flora there exist nearly exclusively yellow flowering Erysimum species. Among these species you find some cultivars that are used as garden plants, e.g. the Siberian Wallflower with its large, orange to yellow blooms. At the end of the bloom time the plants develop up to 10 cm long pods. The genus belongs to the Mustard family and is thus related to the cabbages.

MADEIRA STORK'S BILL
GERANIUM MADERENSE

BLOOM TIME
From March to September

CHARACTERISTICS
The up to 1 m (3,3') tall plant has strongly pinnate, dark green leaves. The lower leaves bow rigidly, rosette-shaped from the long purple stalks to the ground. The single blooms form a dense, spherical shock on the top of the foliage. The well-rounded flowers consist of five pink petals.

SITE:
The Madeira Stork's Bill grows at rocky sites in the upper zones of the laurel forest (up to an altitude of 1500 m/1640 yd.). It is hardly possible to find it in its natural habitat but it is frequently cultivated in gardens and parks, e.g. around Ribeiro Frio.

INTERESTING TO KNOW:
Madeira Stork's Bill resembles the more frequent, also endemic Anemone-leaved Stork's Bill (Geranium palmatum). The latter is more delicate and has orange anthers (in contrast to the red ones of Madeira Stork's Bill). You will find seven other Geranium species. Some of them are also known in Europe, for example the Stinking Stork's Bill (Geranium robertianum). The leaves of the latter smell disagreeably when they are crumbled. The geraniums that are popular as balcony plants belong to the related genus Pelargonium.

MADEIRA TREE FOXGLOVE
ISOPLEXIS SCEPTRUM

BLOOM TIME
Mainly from June to August, often until September

CHARACTERISTICS
The shrub can grow up to 3 m (10') tall. The inflorescences are tall and conspicuously orange. The evergreen, tapered leaves are arranged rosette-like around the twigs.

SITE:
This imposing and attractive plant grows at clear sites in the laurel forest or in the adjoining Heather scrubland. However the plant is very rare in its natural habitat. Today it nearly exclusively grows in steep, practically inaccessible ravines. Beautiful specimens can be contemplated in the parks of Ribeiro Frio and Queimadas. Here and there the Madeira Tree Foxglove feels at home along the levadas.

INTERESTING TO KNOW:
The endemic Madeira Tree Foxglove is a relative of the European Common Foxglove. Both are nearly equally toxic. On the Canary Islands you can find three similar species that do also flower orange. There has been observed that the Tree Foxgloves are pollinated by the indigenous chiffchaff (Phylloscopus collybita). This bird species does not live on Madeira.

COMMON FOXGLOVE,
PURPLE FOXGLOVE
DIGITALIS PURPUREA

BLOOM TIME
From March to September

CHARACTERISTICS
The herbaceous plant grows 0,5-1 m (1,8-3,3') tall. The big, purple flowers are placed next to each other on long stalks. The flowers are spotted on the inside of the corolla. In contrast, the related endemic Madeira Tree Foxglove is larger and flowers orange (cf. p. 141).

SITE:
The Common Foxglove is especially frequent in the laurel forest zone. You can find it at clear sites along the roadsides. It is also spread in those areas where the forest has been cleared already a long time ago, e.g. along the Levada do Paúl or at the southern slope of the Pico Grande. It also thrives in the mountains and can be encountered e.g. on the way from the Pico do Arieiro to the Pico Ruivo.

INTERESTING TO KNOW:
This plant is very poisonous. Anyway it has always been an important medicinal plant in Europe. The leaves contain digitalis glycosides, substances that influence the heart muscle and are thus employed to treat heart diseases. The leaves were usually picked during bloom time. Afterwards the active agents were extracted and adjusted on a certain degree of effectiveness. Today glycosides are produced artificially. The plant is not suitable for self-treatment.

SWEET VIOLET
VIOLA ODORATA

BLOOM TIME
From October to July

CHARACTERISTICS

The dark purple blossoms scent very pleasantly. The leaves are kidney-shaped, more or less hairy, slightly serrated and all placed at the base of the plant. Their dimensions may vary (up to 10 cm (4") long). The leaf-less, 25 cm (22") long flower stalk arises from the leaf rosette.

SITE:
The delicate plant grows exclusively at altitudes higher than 400 m (440 yd.) in the laurel forest and the adjoining areas. It requires shadow and humidity and can be encountered along various levadas, e.g. along the Levada da Serra between Camacha and Portela or along the Levada do Central, above Porto Moniz.

INTERESTING TO KNOW:
The Sweet Violet is also known in Europe where it is one of the first plants to bloom in spring. Botanists grant the status of a proper subspecies (Viola odorata maderensis) to the variation that grows on Madeira and the Canary Islands. The Wood Violet (Viola riviniana) is native to Madeira and Europe. Its blossoms resemble those of the Sweet Violet but do not scent and appear all year round. The leaves are heart-shaped and hairless. They are placed both at the base and at the flower stalk. Ants spread the seeds of both species.

ROCK NAVELWORT
UMBILICUS RUPESTRIS

BLOOM TIME
From April to June

CHARACTERISTICS
The fleshy, carved basal leaves are shield-shaped. The stalk arises from the centre where the leaves are lowered navel-like. The upright, 10-50 cm (4-20") long stalks bear small, kidney-shaped leaves. More than half of the stalk is covered densely with green to white, tubular flowers.

SITE:
The Rock Navelwort requires humid, shady sites. It mainly grows in clefts of rocks or walls. It is widespread in the laurel forest and reaches up to altitudes of more than 1000 m (1100 yd.) e.g. below the Pico Grande or along the way between Eira do Serrado and Curral das Freiras. You may also find the Rock Navelwort at appropriate sites beneath the laurel forest zone.

INTERESTING TO KNOW:
A related species, the Horizontal Navelwort (Umbilicus horizontalis), does also grow on Madeira. Its stalks only bear flowers in the upper third. In contrast to those of the Rock Navelwort, the blooms are nearly stalkless and stick out horizontally. Both species are also spread in the Mediterranean region. The Rock Navelwort thrives even in Western Europe and on the British Isles.

MADEIRA ORCHID,
RICHLY-LEAVED MARSH ORCHID
DACTYLORHIZA FOLIOSA

BLOOM TIME
From May to July

CHARACTERISTICS
The up to 60 cm (24") tall endemic is Madeira's largest wild orchid. It resembles the members of the genus Dactylorhiza that are spread in Europe. The flowers are pink to red, about 2,5 cm (10") broad and grouped in conical, up to 30 cm (12") long inflorescences. The long, narrow leaves withdraw in winter.

SITE:
The plant requires shadow and humidity. In the laurel forest in the north of the island you will most likely find it at altitudes of 600-1000 m (655-1100 yd.). It is quite frequent and thrives along various levadas, e.g. along the Levada do Furado between Ribeiro Frio and Portela or around Queimadas and Rabaçal. Hikers can see it below the southern slope of the Pico Grande or around the Encumeada-Pass. It is planted around the trout farm of Ribeiro Frio.

INTERESTING TO KNOW:
Within the family of wild orchids, botanists distinguish between two similar genera, Orchis (Rock Orchid, cf. p. 167) and Dactylorhiza, by the different nodules. Both are represented on Madeira. If you compare specimens that have not bloomed yet you can observe that the buds of Dactylorhiza species lay open and unprotected since they have sprouted. In contrast, buds of Orchis species are wrapped in the leaf shield.

145

Two-leaved Gennaria
Gennaria diphylla

Bloom time
From December to May

Characteristics

The Two-leaved Gennaria has small, yellowish-green blooms and is thus quite inconspicuous. Each stalk bears up to 40 single blossoms that all turn to the same direction. The 10-20 cm (4-8") tall plant uses to grow in little groups. Each plant has one or two stalkless, heart-shaped leaves.

Site:

The Two-leaved Gennaria is to be found in the lower laurel forest zone at altitudes of 600-900 m (655-985 yd.). It prefers shady, humid sites either in the laurel forest or in the heather scrubland. Hikers can encounter it e.g. along the Levada da Serra above Portela or on the way to the viewpoint Balcões, close to Ribeiro Frio. Several specimens grow along the way from the Eira do Serrado to Curral das Freiras or in the Quinta do Santo da Serra.

Interesting to know:

Besides Madeira, the Two-leaved Gennaria also grows on the Canary Islands, in Morocco, Portugal and in the western Mediterranean region. It is the most frequent of all wild orchid species that occur on Madeira. With about 25000 species, the orchids are the largest family among the flowering plants. Most of them grow in tropical or subtropical regions. It surprises that there are only five species indigenous to Madeira.

146

SPOTTED NEOTINEA,
DENSE-FLOWERED ORCHID
NEOTINEA MACULATA

BLOOM TIME
From April to June

CHARACTERISTICS
Including the inflorescence, the plant is up to 25 cm (10") tall. Numerous, densely growing, white-brownish, nearly closed flowers are placed at the tip of the stalks. They scent of vanilla. The dark spots that are situated in rows on the longish, sharp leaves gave the plant its name.

SITE:
Spotted Neotinea is a quite rare orchid. It prefers altitudes of the laurel forest zone (600-1200 m/655-1310 yd.) but requires certain light. Thus it mainly grows on the southern half of the island in the relatively dry heather scrubland, on mountain pastures or sparsely green embankments. Hikers can encounter it between Boca da Corrida and Pico Grande or between Pico Ruivo and Encumeada-Pass.

INTERESTING TO KNOW:
Besides Madeira, the plant is native to the more humid Canary Islands, the Mediterranean region, the Portuguese and Spanish Atlantic coast and even Ireland. The flowers remain nearly closed, a feature which helps to distinguish Spotted Neotinea from other orchid species. The latter use to have a broad upper bloom part, the labellum. It serves as a mooring point for insects and thus encourages them to pollinate the flower.

147

EUROPEAN CHAIN FERN
WOODWARDIA RADICANS

BLOOM TIME
Spores from April to August

CHARACTERISTICS

The bipinnate, strong fronds are up to 3 m (10') long. The single compounds are about 30 cm (12") long. The spore capsules are placed in two files along the middle rib of each compound. Older fronds develop bulbils at their tips. The plant propagates vegetatively by these bulbils.

SITE:
The European Chain Fern is a typical plant of the laurel forest. It prefers humid and shady sites. It can also thrive at sparser spots, e.g. along roadsides, but stays smaller there. It often populates larger areas in hollows, on rock faces and embankments. You will frequently encounter it.

INTERESTING TO KNOW:
The European Chain Fern is the largest wild growing fern on Madeira. Fossil finds give evidence that it has already been indigenous to Madeira for more than 2 million years. It is a relic species that was even spread in Central Europe under humid, warm conditions during the so-called tertiary (paleogene and lower neogene). The plant is delicate about frost and thus retired during the Ice Age. It survived under milder climatic conditions and is to be found on Madeira, the Canary Islands, the Azores and occasionally in Southern Europe and Northwest Africa.

Canary Island Deer's Foot Fern
Davallia canariensis

Bloom time
None

Characteristics

This very frequent species has 20-40 cm (8-16") long fronds that emerge from a crawling, partly overground, fingerthick rhizome. It is remarkable that they are placed that separately. Both rhizome and stalks are covered with red hairs. The fronds die in summer but sprout again in autumn.

Site:

The Canary Island Deer's Foot Fern is spread both in the laurel forest and in the adjoining heather scrubland. It prefers rocky sites or walls, e.g. along levadas. Occasionally it can grow epiphytically (i.e. on trees, e.g. on the Stinklaurel).

Interesting to know:

Besides all Macaronesian archipelagos (the Azores, Madeira, the Canary Islands, the Cape Verde Islands), the Canary Island Deer's Foot Fern is also native to Morocco and the Iberian Peninsula. Fossil finds in the valley of São Jorge prove that it already populated Madeira together with other species of the laurel forest in the Pliocene (more than 2 million years ago). A remarkable feature are the clearly discernible spore capsules (sori) at the bottom of the fronds. They are placed at the margin of the double compounds and surrounded by bowl-shaped covers.

MAIDENHAIR FERN
ADIANTUM CAPILLUS VENERIS

BLOOM TIME

Evergreen; spores are ripe from July to October

CHARACTERISTICS

The 10-60 cm (4-24") tall Maidenhair Fern is the most delicate of all fern species that grow on Madeira. The light green fronds are double to fourfold pinnate. The thin single compounds are only several millimetres broad and resemble little fans. They are lobed at the upper margin.

SITE:

The Maidenhair Fern is a quite frequent species. It does not tolerate direct sunlight and is thus to be found at shady, often even dark sites in the laurel forest. It populates rock faces at which water is running down constantly or grows close to wells, sources or even in caves.

INTERESTING TO KNOW:

Florists in Western and Central Europe often use it as a decorating supplement. In former times it was employed to treat respiratory diseases. The Maidenhair Fern belongs to the Polypody Fern family that contains more than 200 species that are spread in all warmer regions of the world. The Maidenhair Fern on this picture is also called Common Maidenhair. All Maidenhair species are easy to propagate asexually, either by parting the entire plant or by cutting off root runners. It is considerably more difficult to cultivate ferns out of spores.

KIDNEY-LEAVED MAIDENHAIR FERN
ADIANTUM RENIFORME

BLOOM TIME
None

CHARACTERISTICS

Looking at this 5-20 cm (2-8") plant you will not notice the relations to the Maidenhair Fern (cf. p. 150). The kidney-shaped, quite robust fronds are not subdivided and resemble the leaves of flowering plants. They are identified as fern fronds by the spore capsules at the bottom.

SITE:

The rare Kidney-leaved Maidenhair Fern is mostly found in the laurel forest zone up to an altitude of 1000 m (1100 yd.). It thrives very well at rock faces along the levadas. It is relatively tolerant of dryness and can grow in shady rock clefts even in coastal areas.

INTERESTING TO KNOW:

Besides Madeira, the Kidney-leaved Maidenhair Fern also grows on the Canary Islands and on the Cape Verde Islands. Moreover it thrives in various regions both in West Africa and East Asia and on Madagascar. This peculiar coverage area is due to the fact that ferns, as all spore plants, can more easily extend over large distances than flowering plants. The spores can be passed around for months by wind until they are deposited somewhere and develop to young plants. The heavy seeds of flowering plants lack this ability.

151

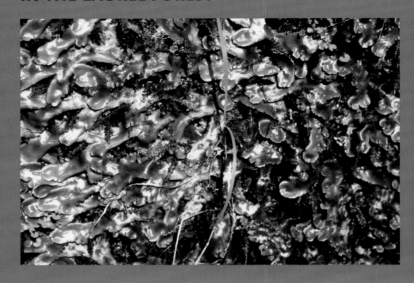

LIVERWORT
HEPATICAE

BLOOM TIME
None

CHARACTERISTICS

Many liverworts have a flat thallus (vegetation tissue) that firmly sticks to the ground or the rock. The thallus consists of winding, often ramified and linked ribbons or stripes that are often crinkled. They are green or reddish. There are also flaking liverworts that lead to mosses.

SITE:

Liverworts do not absorb water by their roots but by their overhead organs and thus require a nearly permanent humidity. The plant is characteristic for a plant society that populates the steep slopes and rock faces of the laurel forest. You can encounter liverworts along many levadas in this area.

INTERESTING TO KNOW:

In former times, liverworts were connected with the liver for their often-reddish colour. Anyway it could not be proven by medicine that the plant cures liver diseases. About 170 Liverwort species are native to Madeira. Together with algae, funguses, lichens and mosses, liverworts belong to the lower plants. On Madeira, more than 1900 lower plant species have been distinguished. Until know it is not certain whether there are any endemic species among them. Detailed researches have not been carried out yet.

OLD MAN'S BEARD
USNEA BARBATA

BLOOM TIME
None

CHARACTERISTICS

Old Man's Beard is an epi-phyte, i.e. it always grows on trees or shrubs where it develops long, greenish-grey beards that hang down from the twigs. The single threads are very ramified. At ripeness, the threads may bear big fruits. They are disc-shaped and have a wreath of lashes.

SITE:

On Madeira, the Old Man's Beard is quite frequent in areas with a high humidity. It is native both to the laurel forest and to the adjoining scrublands and preferably grows on indigenous heather species (Tree Heather, Madeira Green-flowered Heather). Today it can also be found in afforested pine forests.

INTERESTING TO KNOW:

On Madeira you can find about 450 lichen spe-cies. Neither the exact number nor the portion of endemic species is known. Thus they still open up a large area of research to scientists. Anyway, the Old Man's Beard definitely is a cosmopoli-tan. In Europe it grows for example in mountain forests with a high frequency of fog. Old Man's Beard does not do any harm to the host tree. Anyhow it mainly grows on dead wood, i.e. on numb branches below the top of the tree. It absorbs humidity out of the air and obtains nutrients by decomposing the bark of the tree.

On Cliffs and in the Mountains

A heath forest once spread over the plateau Paúl da Serra and on the slopes of the highest mountain peaks. In depressions without outlet it moved on to moor. This type of vegetation reminds of the moors and heaths in West Europe and the British Isles. You can still find signs of moor creation with Peat Moss on Paúl da Serra today. Tree Heather, Madeira Green-flowered Heather, Wax Myrtle, Madeira Juniper and Madeira Bilberry grew in the adjoining forest. They were used for the extraction of firewood or for the production of charcoal. Until about 30 years ago local people still climbed up to Paúl da Serra to extract firewood for using in the kitchen. Later, the deforested areas were used as pasture land for sheep and goats. The remaining heath forests (e.g. at the Bica da Cana and at the Pico Ruivo) are under conservation. There are plans to regenerate other areas. But reforestation is also under way by planting conifers for economical purposes. In the areas around the actual mountain peaks you find extreme climatic conditions. The winter lasts half a year and during this time there are nightly frosts nearly all the days. However, if there is sunshine it can be very hot during daytime. It is not unusual to experience 20 degrees Celsius difference between night and day. Most of the sites are rocky. The topsoil is very thin or does not exist

at all. Only a few plants are able to thrive at these sites. They are often related to the species that grow in the European mountains (the Pyrenees, the Alps, etc.). Many grow rosette-shaped or cushion-like and thus have a relatively small surface. This feature protects them both against evaporation and frostbite. Steep rock faces dry out very rapidly. Plants that populate these sites often have succulent leaves and are thus able to store water for sunnier days.

Rocky sites do also have their particular flora below the highest regions. They do often contain species that are closely related to the inhabitants of the mountain peaks. Several highly specialized species like the Disc Houseleek are able to thrive at rock faces from coastal levels upwards to the highest mountains.

Goats are very good climbers and enabled to pasture even steep rock faces. Until very recently, many thousands have been kept more or less wild in the Madeiran mountains but the delicate flora is often intolerant of being nibbled and was thus severely threatened. Some years ago the pastures have been restricted to fenced in areas. The vegetation at other sites is now able to regenerate. Such an area is crossed by the popular panorama walk from the Pico do Arieiro to the Pico Ruivo, the highest peak. Hikers can also contemplate the flora of the mountains at the Pico Grande.

MADEIRA JUNIPER,
CANARY ISLAND JUNIPER
JUNIPERUS CEDRUS

BLOOM TIME

From December to March; bears berries in spring

CHARACTERISTICS

The up to 10 m (11 yd.) tall conifer develops branches that emerge horizontally from the trunk. Thin twigs with soft, short needles hang down from the branches. The velvet bark is coloured chocolate. The fruits are green at first but later change colour to reddish-brown.

SITE:

The Madeira Juniper is a plant of the mountainous regions. Anyway, it grows at rock faces even in the laurel forest zone. It has become rare in both areas but is frequently cultivated, e.g. around Ribeiro Frio, in Queimadas or in the Jardim Tropical Monte Palace.

INTERESTING TO KNOW:

On Madeira, the berries were once used by traditional medicine (pain-relieving and sudorific). They were not used as spices. Due to deforestation, the once frequent tree was already severely decimated in the 15th/16th century. The strong wood is not eaten by insects and was thus for example employed to construct the carved ceiling of the cathedral of Funchal. On Madeira, the Madeira Juniper is one of only a few conifers that have been enabled by nature to survive against the faster growing deciduous trees. It also grows on the Canary Islands.

TREE HEATHER
ERICA ARBOREA

BLOOM TIME
From March to May

CHARACTERISTICS
The close relative of the Bog Heather (Erica tetralix) is an up to 5 m (5,5 yd.) tall tree with a thick trunk. It develops masses of whitish, inconspicuous blooms. The leaves are darker than those of the Madeira Green-flowered Heather (cf. p. 126). Young twigs are covered with white hairs.

SITE:
In former times the frost tolerant species of Tree Heather and Madeira Green-flowered Heather used to form forests on mountain peaks above the laurel forest zone. At sparse sites and on dry mountain ridges Tree Heather can also thrive down to an altitude of 400m (440 yd.). You can find greater populations around the Pico Ruivo and Bica da Cana. Some of the specimens that grow there are several centuries old.

INTERESTING TO KNOW:
The Tree Heather has a high fuel value and burns odourless. Madeira's mountain region was common property for a long time. That means that everyone was allowed to get firewood there. The simple folk did not heat but used the wood to fuel ovens and stoves. Charcoal burner was a widespread profession. Charcoal was mainly extracted from Tree Heathers; thus the tree is quite rare in its natural habitat today.

Madeira Bilberry
Vaccinium padifolium

Bloom time

From May to July; bears fruits from August to October

Characteristics

The Madeira Bilberry is several metres tall. Apart from its growth it is very similar to European Bilberry species. The small, serrated leaves are placed spirally around reddish twigs. The dark blue berries develop out of bell-shaped blooms. These are white with pink spots.

Site:

In the central mountainous regions you will find the Madeira Bilberry as a characteristic plant of the native heather forests. The foliage of specimens that grow at these sites turns red in winter because of the nightly frost. Madeira Bilberry also thrives at sparse, dry sites in the laurel forest where it stays evergreen. Hikers can encounter it along the levadas around Ribeiro Frio, Queimadas and Rabaçal. It is also frequent along the road that leads from the Poiso-Pass to the Pico do Arieiro.

Interesting to know:

Madeira Bilberry is an endemic species. The fruits are edible but hardly not consumed by the indigenous population because they taste quite sour. Pudim de uva da serra (bilberry pudding) is occasionally served as a dessert. The berries are traditionally used to prepare a jam that is employed to treat cough and colds.

Pride of Madeira, Madeira Viper's Bugloss Echium candicans

Bloom Time
From May to July

Characteristics

This attractive flowering plant resembles the Splendid Viper's Bugloss (cf. p. 65). Anyway, the candle-shaped inflorescences are significantly narrower, sharper and about 30 cm (12") long. The numerous blooms are strong purple to dark blue. The entire shrub is up to 1,5 m (5') tall.

Site:

At altitudes higher than 800 m (875 yd.), the Pride of Madeira grows at rocky slopes in the laurel forest, e.g. at the slope between Eira do Serrado and Curral das Freiras or below the Pico Grande. You can also find it around the highest peaks, e.g. along the way from the Pico do Arieiro to the Pico Ruivo. It frequently grows along roadsides, e.g. between Serra de Água and Encumeada or in parks, e.g. in Ribeiro Frio and Queimadas.

Interesting to know:

Pride of Madeira is supposed to be the most beautiful of all endemic flowering plants on Madeira. In many exotic countries, British scientists invented similar denominations for the local "national plant", i.e. for the most beautiful endemic plant. Another Viper's Bugloss is the national plant of Tenerife. You can also find a Pride of Bolivia, a Pride of Barbados and a Pride of Trinidad.

WHITE EVERLASTING FLOWER,
WHITE STRAWFLOWER
HELICHRYSUM MELALEUCUM

BLOOM TIME

From March to June,
occasionally up to August

CHARACTERISTICS

The small shrub belongs to the compound flowers and reaches up to 0,5 m (1,8") tall. The felty, hairy, grey to green leaves are narrow, tapered and do only have one leaf vein. The small blooms are white with a black spot in the centre. Each flower stalk bears several blooms.

SITE:

The White Everlasting Flower populates rocky sites in central regions of the island, e.g. along the way from the Pico do Arieiro to the Pico Ruivo. It is also to be found on rocky slopes at the northern coast. Two related, also endemic species are restricted to the rocky coastal areas (up to an altitude of 150 m/165 yd.): the Conical Everlasting Flower (Helichrysum obconicum) has elliptical leaves and yellow blooms. The rare Lourenço Everlasting Flower (Helichrysum devium) resembles the White Everlasting Flower but has got leaves with three veins. The flowers gleam pink with a purple spot.

INTERESTING TO KNOW:

The flowers of Everlasting Flowers do not wilt and have thus always been employed to weave flower wreaths in the Mediterranean regions. On Madeira, the participants in the vow-procession on the 1st of May put on wreaths that are made of the blossoms of the White Everlasting Flower.

WALL ROCK CRESS
ARABIS CAUCASICA

BLOOM TIME
From March to July

CHARACTERISTICS
The up to 20 cm (8") tall plant belongs to the cruciferous plants. These plants have four petals that are organized cross-like. The pale green leaves are longish and have serrated margins. Thin stalks emerge from leave rosettes. Each of them bears several white, scenting flowers.

SITE:
The Wall Rock Cress populates rock faces from an altitude of 200 m (220 yd.) upwards but is most likely to be found in the mountains. It is quite frequent along the way from the Boca da Corrida to the Pico Grande. It is spread in entire South Europe, the Canary Islands and the Near East.

INTERESTING TO KNOW:
It is debatable whether Arabis caucasica belongs to the indigenous Madeiran flora or not. Perhaps it was introduced as an ornamental plant and went wild afterwards. It is very difficult to distinguish from the very similar Arabis alpina that thrives in the Alps and reaches up to an altitude of 3000 m (3280 yd.). There are also some related species in Western and Central Europe: the Tower Rock Cress (Arabis glabra) and the Hairy Rock Cress (Arabis hirsuta). Both belong to the attractive dry grassland flora. They require chalky soils and are quite rare.

MADEIRA SAXIFRAGE, MADEIRA BREAKSTONE
SAXIFRAGA MADERENSIS

BLOOM TIME
From April to June

CHARACTERISTICS

The flat cushion plant is at most 15 cm (6") tall. The small, semicircular leaves are strongly lobed. They form a dense foliage from which emerge numerous, thin flower stalks. Several small, white and five-petaled blooms are placed upon each of them.

SITE:

The Madeira Saxifrage populates cracks in rock faces, i.e. sites that are scarcely inhabited by other plants. It is a typical plant of the mountainous regions and to be found e.g. along the panorama way from the Pico do Arieiro to the Pico Ruivo. However, it also thrives in lower regions (down to 500 m/547 yd. altitude), e.g. along the old mountain trail between Eira do Serrado and Curral das Freiras.

INTERESTING TO KNOW:

The flat cushion plant is endemic to Madeira. Covered by a blanket of snow the plant can even support strong frost. For its small surface it will not dry out when being exposed to strong sunlight and growing on freezing soils at the same time. The closest relatives grow in the Pyrenees, on Corsica and in the Alps where they reach the highest altitudes that could be populated by flowering plants. The common name of the genus refers to its rocky habitat.

Madeira Violet
Viola paradoxa

Bloom time
From April to July

Characteristics

The cushion-like plant has often a woody base and grows up to 20 cm (8") tall. It develops numerous shining yellow blossoms and thus reminds of yellow Pansies. The lower of the five petals has a little spore. The numerous leaves are grey to green and narrow.

Site:

The endemic Madeira Violet is characteristic of the flora of the mountains. It is restricted to rocky sites at altitudes higher than 1600 m (1750 yd.). Since the usage of these areas as pastureland has been reduced, hikers can often encounter the Madeira Violet along the way from the Pico do Arieiro to the Pico Ruivo. Those who do not hike can find it cultivated as a pot plant around the trout farm of Ribeiro Frio.

Interesting to know:

The botanical denomination "paradoxa" is due to the yellow blooms of the Madeira Violet. Most other violet species flower violet. The Scorpion Violet (Viola scorpiuroides) is a similar species of the Eastern Mediterranean regions. It also blooms yellow and grows cushion-like. The yellow Pansy (cf. Characteristics) is a cultivated form that descends from the Yellow Violet (Viola lutea), a species from the Alps.

DISC HOUSELEEK
AEONIUM GLANDULOSUM

BLOOM TIME
From April to June

CHARACTERISTICS
This member of the Stonecrop family develops plate-like, about 20 cm (8") broad rosettes. They seem to adhere to rock faces and grow conically into the air before bloom time. Later, the outer leaves turn red. Up to 25 cm (10") tall inflorescences with numerous, yellow single blooms emerge from the cones.

SITE:
The Disc Houseleek is endemic to Madeira and a very flexible plant. It populates sites from sea level upwards to mountainous regions. Especially beautiful specimens are to be found at the north-western steep coast between São Vicente and Porto Moniz or below the Pico das Torres along the so-called tunnel-way from the Pico do Arieiro to the Pico Ruivo.

INTERESTING TO KNOW:
Only a few plants are able to populate steep rock faces. The roots extract the often rare water and the nutrients from clefts in the rock. With its succulent (water saving) leaves, the Disc Houseleek is adapted to dryness. Through its rosette-like shape the Disc Houseleek minimizes its surface and thus the evaporation. The flat growth protects the plant against the destructive force of the water that often runs down the rocks heavily after rainfalls.

Viscid Houseleek
Aeonium glutinosum

Bloom time
From May to September

Characteristics

The Viscid Houseleek develops rosettes of succulent (water saving), spatula-like, sticky leaves. Each plant has various rosettes that are placed upon woody stalks and thus resembles a little shrub. A long flower stalk with many star-shaped, yellow blossoms emerges from each rosette.

Site:

As the related Disc Houseleek (cf. p. 164), the Viscid Houseleek grows at rock faces. Both species often occur together, e.g. at the steep slopes of the northern coast. The Viscid Houseleek surpasses only scarcely an altitude of 800 m (875 yd.) and is often cultivated in gardens, mainly on walls, at average altitudes.

Interesting to know:

The genus Aeonium is related to the Stonecrop and the Houseleek but is nearly restricted to the Atlantic Islands. There are known about 40 Aeonium species: 35 are endemic to the Canary Islands, two to Madeira and two to the Cape Verde Islands. Today they are all under international protection of species because of their small distribution area. Members of this genus are likely to hybridise. On Madeira you can also find a hybrid of the two endemic species. Its growth is similar to the Viscid Houseleek but it has stickier leaves with brown stripes.

DOWNY STONECROP
AICHRYSON VILLOSUM

BLOOM TIME
From April to July

CHARACTERISTICS

This tiny member of the Stonecrop family (5-10 cm/2-4") has spoon-shaped leaves that change colour to red around bloom time. The star-shaped flowers are strongly yellow; the centre is often darker than the wreath of petals. The flowers are 1,2-1,5 cm (0,5-0,6") in diameter.

SITE:
The Downy Stonecrop populates rock faces at all altitudes that are mainly free of frost (up to an altitude of 1300 m/1420yd.). It is to be found both in coastal areas and mountainous regions.

INTERESTING TO KNOW:
The Downy Stonecrop is endemic to Madeira and the Azores. The similar Madeira Stonecrop (Aichryson divaricatum) is restricted to Madeira. It is taller (up to 30 cm/12"), has more elongated leaves and smaller blooms (6-8 mm/0,24-0,32"). It flowers from June onwards and also populates rock faces but nearly exclusively occurs in the laurel forest zone (400-1000 m/440-1100 yd.). Both Aichryson species also grow on trunks and branches of Stinklaurel trees. In the shady forests, this "epiphytical" lifestyle enables them to reach more easily up to the rare light. Otherwise you will only find epiphytical flowering plants in the tropical rain forests, mainly orchids and bromelias.

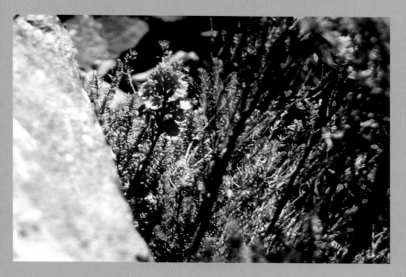

ROCK ORCHID
ORCHIS SCOPULORUM

BLOOM TIME
May and June

CHARACTERISTICS

The 20-40 cm (8-16") tall Rock Orchid is a very rare, wild growing orchid that reminds of orchid species that are spread in Central Europe. The irregular, about 9 cm (3,6") long and 6 cm (2,4") broad inflorescences consist of pink flowers. The Madeira Orchid (cf. p. 145) is a more frequent species.

SITE:

The Rock Orchid is an exclusive mountain inhabitant and grows in the areas around the highest mountain peaks, up to an altitude of more than 1800 m (1970 yd.). At rock faces you can also encounter it below the laurel forest zone, e.g. below the viewing point Balcões close to Ribeiro Frio. The plant requires a certain humidity and is delicate about being nibbled. Thus it will not last close to pasturing sheep and goats.

INTERESTING TO KNOW:

Until now, Rock Orchid has been regarded as an endemic to Madeira. Anyway, some scientists assume that it simply is an endemic subspecies of the Early Purple Orchid (Orchis mascula), a rare species that is to be found on La Palma, in Central Europe and in Northwest Africa. The common name refers to its rocky habitat while the botanical denomination goes back to the testicle-shaped nodules.

Useful Plants

What goes for ornamental plants is also valid for useful plants: They have been imported from all over the world, often already in the times of the great discovery journeys. Madeira was often used as an interchange between the Old and the New World. For example the Sugar Cane, native to Asia, was firstly introduced to Madeira and cultivated successfully. Passing the Canary Islands it was later brought to America by Christopher Columbus. Today, America is one of the principal areas of cultivation of Sugar Cane. And there are many examples like that, also concerning plants that appear so ordinary as the wheat does. It has been brought to Brazil over Madeira and the Cape Verde Islands. But we do also find plants that were brought from America to Madeira, e.g. the Custard Apple, the Passion Fruit, the Guava and the Surinam Cherry. Among other delicate, tropical fruits they could be established on Madeira but never were cultivated successfully in Europe.

Sugar cane, vine and bananas, the so called "culturas ricas" (rich cultures) were always of a special economic value. Today, the export of sugar cane has lost all of its importance. However, vine and bananas have maintained their status as the most important export goods and take up the best cultivation grounds. Areas that are less suitable for cultivation have always been used for growing plants that are used to feed the population: wheat, maize, potatoes, sweet potatoes, taro and various types of vegetables. These plants have to be grown by hand due to the site conditions. The cultivation is constantly declining today because it often results cheaper to import goods than to produce them on the island. Many farmers do traditionally cultivate for their personal needs. On these little agricultural parcels you will often find plants that may be known in Europe but are only scarcely or not at all (no longer) eaten there. Examples are the Portuguese Cabbage or the Lupine.

Tropical fruits are not such an important component of the Madeiran diet as you may suppose according to common assumptions. They have always been very expensive and thus eaten mainly by rich families. Monasteries, British wine merchants and other owners of large estates did cultivate exotic fruit trees in their gardens. They did only spread to kitchen gardens and little plantations when tourism began to be an important part of the Madeiran economy and were mainly grown to supply hotels. Until today tropical fruits are mostly produced in private gardens as a sideline for the respective owner. Specialized merchants, hotels and restaurants buy the papayas, avocados, mangos, loquats, tree tomatoes, etc.

SWEET CHESTNUT TREE
CASTANEA SATIVA

BLOOM TIME
June and July

CHARACTERISTICS

The about 15 m (16,5 yd.) tall tree has a whitish bark. The narrow, tapered leaves are up to 20 cm (8") long and serrated. The tiny, yellowish blooms are placed in long, narrow catkins. The prickly fruits ripen in autumn. They contain one to three "chestnuts" that resemble nuts and have a brown shell.

SITE:
The Sweet Chestnut Tree is a frequent tree at altitudes of 400-1000 m (440-1100 yd.). It often lines levadas, e.g. the Levada da Serra close to Camacha or the Levada do Caniçal close to Machico. You can encounter large forests around Curral das Freiras and above Jardim da Serra.

INTERESTING TO KNOW:
The Sweet Chestnut Tree was introduced to Madeira from Southern Europe. The tree grows in the foggy zones above the agriculturally used parcels and was thus not in competition with the "culturas ricas" (literally: rich cultures): sugar cane and vines. The starchy chestnuts were an important food for the poorer farmers in higher regions and a satiating component in the daily stew. The Madeirans also use sweet chestnuts to prepare cakes and to produce a liqueur. Visitors can still try both specialities in Curral das Freiras.

CUSTARD APPLE TREE
ANNONA CHERIMOLA

BLOOM TIME

From May to July; bears ripe fruits in the winter months and in early spring

CHARACTERISTICS

The up to 10 m (11 yd.) tall tree has oversized, ovate leaves that hang conspicuously down. The plump, heart-shaped fruits are of a cone-like, scaly style. The shell is dark green to purple-brown and leathery. They can reach more than 15 cm (6") in diameter but often stay apple-sized.

SITE:

The Custard Apple Tree thrives both in the north and in the south of the island from the coast up to an altitude of about 400 m (440 yd.). It is often cultivated in private gardens, occasionally in little plantations, and mainly to be found in the outskirts of Funchal, in Faial and in Santana.

INTERESTING TO KNOW:

The Custard Apple Tree is native to the highlands of Peru and Ecuador and can thus also be cultivated at chillier latitudes and even in Spain. From there it is currently exported to other European countries. On Madeira, it is only cultivated for the island's needs. The fruit can be stored several days in its hard, unripe state. It is ripe as soon as the shell can be crushed easily. Ripe fruits rot rapidly and should thus be eaten soon. The white pulp has a consistency that is similar to pears but has a more delicate taste. The fruit is spooned up. The large, black pips are not eaten.

Avocado Tree, Alligator Pear
Persea americana

Bloom time

From January to April; bears ripe fruits in the summer and in early autumn

Characteristics

The up to 12 m (13 yd.) tall tree belongs to the Laurel family. The laurel-like, leathery leaves are quite big. The twigs bear panicles of small, inconspicuous blooms at their tips. Solid, pear-shaped fruits hang down from long stalks. The colour varies from green to purple brown.

Site:

The Avocado Tree thrives both in the south (e.g. in the suburbs of Funchal) and in the north (e.g. around Faial) up to an altitude of about 350 m (385 yd.). It either grows in little plantations or as a specimen tree in private gardens. Several beautiful specimens are to be found in the Botanical Garden, Funchal.

Interesting to know:

The Avocado Tree is native to tropical regions in Central and South America where it has already been cultivated in pre-Columbian days. The English and also the Portuguese denomination (abacate) derives from the Indian word "auacatal". The Aztec did not only eat the fruits but also used them for skin care. The fruits are ripe as soon as the skin gives way elastically when pressurizing it. The soft pulp is usually eaten freshly. Restaurants serve the fruits as a hors d'oevre, squeezing either vinaigrette or Madeiran vine on them.

MANGO TREE
MANGIFERA INDICA

BLOOM TIME

From November to May; fruits come to the market in October

CHARACTERISTICS

On Madeira, the Mango Tree uses to be only 3-6 m (10-20') tall. It has a dense crown and long, narrow leaves. Young leaves are red and hang down feebly. Each of the cone-shaped panicles contains up to 3000 tiny, pale yellow blooms. The fruits are kidney-shaped and hang on stalks.

SITE:

On Madeira, the delicate plant only thrives at very sheltered sites near to the southern coast. A large mango plantation is to be found in Fajã dos Padres. Otherwise you can find single specimens in private gardens, e.g. in Lugar de Baixo. In Funchal you can encounter Mango Trees for example in the Quinta Vigia or in the Botanical Garden.

INTERESTING TO KNOW:

The Mango Tree originates from India where it was already cultivated 4000 years ago. The Mango is one of the most important tropical fruits and highly estimated for its vitamin and protein content. On Madeira, the indigenous mangos are sold on the markets in autumn. They are mainly small, orange to yellow fruits with fibrous pulp. The larger, not fibrous sort that is also known in Europe is offered all year round. However, the greater part of the latter is imported to Madeira from South America.

LOQUAT, JAPANESE PLUM
ERIOBOTRYA JAPONICA

BLOOM TIME

From October to December; on Madeira it bears ripe fruits approx. from February onwards

CHARACTERISTICS

The about 6 m (6,5 yd.) tall tree has elliptical, coarse, shining leaves. They are subdivided by distinctive leaf veins. The pale yellow blooms are placed on hairy stalks and form dense panicles. Numerous, orange-yellow, plum-sized fruits with a velvet skin develop from the flowers.

SITE:

The Loquat Tree grows up to an altitude of 800 m (875 yd.) in the south of Madeira; in the north it only reaches up to an altitude of 400 m (440 yd.). You will usually find it as a specimen tree in private gardens or in mixed plantations together with Avocado Trees and Custard Apple Trees. Parts of the Levada do Central (above Porto Moniz) are lined by Loquat Trees.

INTERESTING TO KNOW:

The tree is indigenous to Japan but is nowadays cultivated worldwide in the subtropics. Outside the areas of cultivation you will scarcely find the delicate fruits freshly on the market. The tasty, sweet-sour fruits are eaten raw and with the skin but without the seeds. The related Medlar (Mespilus germanica) was once cultivated in the wine-growing areas of Central Europe. Today it is not used anymore because the woody fruits only become palatable when they are already beginning to rot.

PAPAYA TREE
CARICA PAPAYA

BLOOM TIME

From May to August; bears ripe fruits from June to October

CHARACTERISTICS

The 3-6 m (10-20") tall tree has a thin, scarred, mostly not ramified trunk. The tip of the trunk bears a wreath of long leave stalks. The leaves are parted hand-like; the fingers are strongly lobed. The melon-like fruits develop below the leave wreath and mostly grow directly from the trunk.

SITE:

The Papaya Tree and the Dwarf Banana (cf. p. 180) have similar demands towards their sites. Papaya Trees are thus often to be found on or beside banana plantations, e.g. west of Funchal or in the sheltered valleys of the southwest coast. Occasionally they are also cultivated in the north of the island.

INTERESTING TO KNOW:

The Papaya Tree is native to tropical America where it was already cultivated in pre-Columbian days. The fruits ripen in summer and weigh up to several kilos. They are consumed raw. To eat them one has to halve them, then to remove the black, slimy seeds from the inner cavity and finally to cut the yellow pulp in slices. The shell is not eaten; the fruit is very rich in vitamins but poor in acids. Lemon juice may improve the taste of the fruit. The small papayas with orange pulp that are imported from Brazil to Madeira off-seasonally are more aromatic.

SURINAM CHERRY
EUGENIA UNIFLORA

BLOOM TIME
From December to February

CHARACTERISTICS

The 5 m (5,5 yd.) tall, evergreen tree has numerous ovate, tapered leaves. Several long filaments protrude from each of the little, white blooms. The orange to red fruits are cherry-sized and eightfold ribbed lengthways. The dried flowers hang down from the lower part of the fruit.

SITE:

Up to an altitude of 350 m (385 yd.) the plant is cultivated in many gardens, mainly in the south of Madeira. There are no proper plantations. In Funchal you can encounter the plant for example in the Quinta das Cruzes or in the Botanical Garden.

INTERESTING TO KNOW:

The Surinam Cherry is native to the tropical rain forests of South America (Brazil, Surinam). The soft, sour tasting fruits (port. pitangas) can be consumed raw. They are eaten with the skin but without the seeds. Pitangas are highly perishable and thus cannot be exported. On Madeira, the Surinam Cherry is usually cultivated in private gardens for one's personal use. Around Easter you can find a small amount of fruits on the markets of Funchal and Ribeira Brava. They are sold at high prices to the tourists. The sale of pitanga jam has begun recently.

GUAVA TREE
PSIDIUM GUAJAVA

BLOOM TIME

May and June; bears fruits
from October to January

CHARACTERISTICS

The small tree is 4 m (4.4 yd.)
tall and has longish leaves
with upwards-curved margins.
The leaf veins protrude visibly.
The spherical fruits develop
from white blooms with
numerous, yellow stamens. At
maturity they are pale yellow
and about 5 cm (2") in diameter. The pulp is salmon pink.

SITE:

You can find Guava Trees occasionally in gardens and little plantations up to an altitude of
200 m (220 yd.). They are mainly to be found
in the outer districts of Funchal and in some
coastal towns in the southwest (e.g. Lugar
de Baixo, Ponta do Sol, Madalena do Mar).

INTERESTING TO KNOW:

The Guava (port. goiaba) is native to tropical America. Already in the 16th century it
was brought from Brazil to the Old World by
Portuguese seafarers. The tree spread rapidly in Africa and Asia for its fruits that are
rich in vitamins. It is said that Guavas were
already served at the court of the Indian
Grand Mogul in 1590. The fruits can be eaten
raw with the slightly waxy skin and the pips.
However, the pips are quite solid. The taste
reminds of quinces. The Madeirans use to prepare a jam out of the fruits or make a bombe
glacée of guava purée, cream and sugar.

TREE TOMATO
CYPHOMANDRA BETACEA

BLOOM TIME

From March to June; bears fruits from December to February

CHARACTERISTICS

The Tree Tomato resembles the related Tomato for its crooked twigs and stature but is much taller (up to 4 m/4,4 yd.). The big leaves are heart-shaped and sharp. The scenting, star-like blossoms are green to white. One or more of the ovate, red fruits hang down from each of the long stalks.

SITE:

You will find the Tree Tomato growing here and there in gardens or smaller plantations mainly in the more humid, chillier north of the island. It grows up to an altitude of 600 m (655 yd.). The main areas of cultivation are São Roque do Faial, Santana and São Jorge.

INTERESTING TO KNOW:

The Tree Tomato is native to South America. In the Andes it thrives up to an altitude of 2500 m (2735 yd.). Today it is cultivated in many tropical and subtropical countries. On Madeira, the island's needs are met by cultivation in places. There is no export. The fruits (port. tomate inglés) are rich in vitamins and sold on the markets. Although they resemble tomatoes they taste completely different. The sweet-sour, slightly bitter pulp is spooned out; the leathery skin is unpalatable. On Madeira there is also lemonade and jam made of the fruits. By contrast they are pickled piquantly in South America.

COMMON OSIER, BASKET WILLOW
SALIX VIMINALIS

BLOOM TIME
April and May; harvest in March

CHARACTERISTICS
In cultivation, the trunk of the Common Osier is kept shortly and scarcely surpasses a height of 50 cm (20"). Up to 2,5 m (10') long, very erect growing branches sprout from the trunk. They change colour to reddish in winter. The harvest takes places in March.

SITE:
Common Osier is mainly cultivated in the humid valleys north of Camacha and in the northeast and north of the island. Single specimens are to be found around Curral das Freiras.

INTERESTING TO KNOW:
The plant is native to Europe and was introduced to Madeira because the endemic Canary Willow (Salix canariensis) is not suitable for basket-making. At the end of the 19th century the production of basketwork furniture became an important export good in Camacha. The cultivation of Common Osier was the basis of many farmer's livelihood in the more humid, chillier zones. Today the indigenous basket-makers are not able to cope with the competition from East Europe and Asia. The cultivation of Common Osier has been declining considerably since the beginning of the 1990ies. Today there is no considerable export of wickerwork articles and the sale is nearly exclusively restricted to the island.

DWARF BANANA
MUSA PARADISIACA CAVENDISHII

BLOOM TIME
All year round

CHARACTERISTICS
The trunk of the 5 m (5,5 yd.) tall plant does not consist of wood but is composed of leaf stalks. The big leaves are often slashed by wind. The long, hanging inflorescence has male blooms at the bottom and females at the top. They scent sweetish and are covered by large, purple bracts.

SITE:
Although the cultivation has been declining since 1990, there are still many banana plantations on Madeira. The Dwarf Banana thrives best at sheltered sites at the southwest coast, up to an altitude of 200 m (220 yd.). Occasionally it grows up to an altitude of 300 m (330 yd.) and even in the north of the island. The best areas of cultivation are west of Funchal, in Lugar de Baixo and in Madalena do Mar.

INTERESTING TO KNOW:
The Dwarf Banana is native to China where it is pollinated by bats. On Madeira the bananas develop without pollination from the ovaries of the female blossoms. The plant propagates from root runners. The secondary plant grows up while the fruits of the primary plant are ripening. The perennial and the weaker shoots are cut off after the harvest. The strongest secondary plant will provide the next harvest approximately 12-15 months later.

SUGAR CANE
SACCHARUM OFFICINARUM

BLOOM TIME
From January to March;
on Madeira the plant only
flowers very rarely

CHARACTERISTICS
The up to 2 m (6,6') tall grass
develops dense tufts of maize-
like, sharp-edged leaves. In
contrast to reed, a similar,
very frequent plant, several
stalks emerge from each of
the roots. Most kinds of Cane
Sugar have conspicuously purple stalks. They contain mar-
row with approx. 15% sugar.

SITE:
Sugar Cane is mainly cultivated in the
southwest of Madeira, around Calheta
and Ponta do Sol. However you can also
find it in the northeast around Porto da
Cruz, in Faial and in the valley of Machico.

INTERESTING TO KNOW:
Sugar Cane is native to tropical Asia. Intents to
cultivate it in the Mediterranean region failed.
In 1425 it was finally introduced to Madeira.
Portugal rapidly obtained the monopoly on
the sugar trade in Europe. Anyway, this boom
already came to an end in the middle of the
16th century after Sugar Cane had been introduced to America. Today there is no sugar
production taking place on Madeira. Three
small fabrics produce sugar syrup (port. Mel de
Cana) and rum (port. Aguardente de Cana). The
syrup is used for baking, e.g. for the Bolo de Mel
("honey cake"). The schnapps is an ingredient
of Poncha, a cocktail of lemon juice and honey.

BANANA PASSION FLOWER
PASSIFLORA TRIPARTITA

BLOOM TIME
From April to November

CHARACTERISTICS

The creeper develops an up to 20 m (22 yd.) long shoot that climbs trees and shrubs. The big, hanging flowers consist of a wreath of strongly pink coloured petals. A three-part style protrudes from the centre of the flower. The yellow fruits resemble little bananas.

SITE:
The Banana Passion Flower thrives best in the more humid north of the island where it often goes wild along the lower border of the laurel forest, e.g. along the Levada do Central above Porto Moniz. In the south of the island it grows along the levadas at altitudes of 500-700 m (547-765 yd.).

INTERESTING TO KNOW:
The plant is native to the Andes. The inner part of the fruit is edible (port. Maracujá Banana). The fruit is halved and sucked or spooned out. The pips that are embedded in the pulp are also eaten. The fruits are often sold on markets. They are also used to prepare pudding (pudim de maracujá). The fruits of the related Purple Passion Flower (Passiflora edulis) are more aromatic. You can see it here and there climbing on walls in cultivated land. Its fruits are round and brownish-purple. They are often sold in shrivelled state when the inner part is fully ripe.

Green Taro, Elephant's Ear
Colocasia esculenta

Bloom time

May and June; however, the plant only scarcely develops flowers

Characteristics

The herbaceous plant has giant, up to 50 cm (20") broad, shield-like leaves with thick leaf veins. The about 1 m (3,3') long leaf stalks emerge directly from the thick, nodule-like rhizome. The rhizome is about 10 cm (4") in diameter and can weigh several kilos.

Site:

Green Taro is cultivated mainly at very humid sites up to an altitude of about 700 m (765 yd.). For their humid and sultry climate it also prospers in the undergrowth of banana plantations. It is more frequent in the north than in the south of Madeira. Wild growing specimens are to be found beside sources and brooks.

Interesting to know:

Although they are not closer related, the Green Taro is often mixed up with the Yam. The former is native to India and has already been cultivated in Asia for 2000 years. Today there are about 1000 variations in the tropics and subtropics. Taro (port. Inhame) was once an important basic food. The starchy nodules taste very mild but contain oxalates, which irritate the mucous membranes of mouth and stomach and only become edible after a long cooking time. The cooking water should be replaced several times. Taro is occasionally offered as a side dish for tuna.

PORTUGUESE CABBAGE,
PORTUGUESE KALE
BRASSICA OLERACEA ACEPHALA

BLOOM TIME
All year round

CHARACTERISTICS

This about 1 m (3,3') tall cabbage species resembles the much more delicate Brussels sprouts. However, the strong trunk does not develop sprouts. The coarse leaves are smooth and green. As long as the buds are still closed the long flower stalks look like tender broccoli.

SITE:
Farmers usually cultivate the Portuguese Cabbage on small terraces together with potatoes, sweet potatoes, maize or similar field fruits. On the southern half of the island it thrives at altitudes of 400-800 m (440-875 yd.), in the north it even grows in coastal areas. You can find it most likely at sites that are too foggy and too chilly for more demanding species.

INTERESTING TO KNOW:
The leathery leaves need to be cooked for a long time and thus are cut in very thin slices. In supermarkets they are even sold in an already cut form. The leaves are a principal ingredient of the "Caldo Verde" (green soup), a national dish that is often eaten on Madeira. The entire leaves are used to prepare stews. The tender flower stalks and buds provide a popular side dish. Besides Portugal this species is only cultivated in Northwest Spain and on the Canary Islands.

WHITE SWEET-SCENTED LUPINE
LUPINUS ALBUS

BLOOM TIME
In spring

CHARACTERISTICS

The herbaceous plant grows up to 50 cm (20") tall and has pinnate, slightly hairy leaves. The typical pea flowers (similar to those of broom plants) are organized in candle-shaped, 10-20 cm (4-8") long racemes. They scent pleasantly and are white, sometimes with a bluish tip.

SITE:
Both the White Sweet-scented Lupine and the Yellow Sweet-scented Lupine (Lupinus luteus) are cultivated on small terraces. You can find them along many levadas that cross cultivated land.

INTERESTING TO KNOW:
The wild forms that are native to the Mediterranean region contain bitter alkaloids and are toxic. The bitter principles could be removed in cultivation. In Western and Central Europe, Lupines are planted to improve the soil quality (they bind nitrogen) and as cattle feed. However, the seeds (port. tremoços) are eaten in Portugal. They are yellow, rounded and about 1 cm (0,4") in diameter. You can buy them parboiled in supermarkets. The Madeirans use to pickle them in oil, vinegar, parsley, paprika and garlic. They accompany beer or wine in simple pubs. The thin, solid shell is edible. Anyway, the indigenous population uses to remove them with the teeth.

GARDENS AND PARKS

Besides Madeira there is probably no place in the world where you can find that many interesting parks that are open to the public. Most of them are located in and around Funchal. The capital has always been the centre of the political and economic activities on Madeira. It attracted Portuguese landowners, Flemish and Italian sugar merchants and British wine merchants who resided in the city. Later the tourists have followed them.

Until today about three-quarters of all visitors live in the hotels of Funchal, though nowadays there are comfortable accomodations in almost all parts of the island. Moreover, the especially mild climate of the capital offers perfect conditions to the delicate tropical plants that Madeira became famous for: thus you can contemplate some of the most beautiful gardens in Funchal. Exotic plants first decorated monastery gardens and inner courtyards of palaces. In the 18th and 19th century, mainly the British wine merchants began to lay out their famous Quintas at the verge of the city or in higher located villages like Monte, Camacha and Santo da Serra. Outstanding parks surrounded these Quintas, being the pride of their owners. At the end of the 19th century they were joined by splendid hotel gardens. In the 20th century the garden culture was somehow "democratised". Today, many parks are owned by the public authorities and continuously replenished (Jardim Bôtanico, Quinta das Cruzes, Quinta Magnólia, city parks of Funchal, Quinta do Santo da Serra, Queimadas etc.) One of the most magnificent gardens of Madeira is the Jardim Tropical Monte Palace. It goes back to the extensive park of a venerable hotel and has been developed by a native businessman to its current state. The reestablishment of the Quinta Jardins do Imperador in Monte is due to another private association. The last Austrian emperor lived here in exile in 1922, though the garden existed already in the 19th century. Other estates like the Palheiro Gardens and the Quinta Palmeira are still owned by British families but can be visited. You can also visit several private orchid gardens (Jardim Orquídea, Quinta da Boa Vista, etc.) that are mainly dedicated to cultivate pot and cut flowers both for the selling on the island and the export.

Not least of all there is the forest management that endeavours to lay out some parks in the mountains and in the forests. Apart from the Parque Florestal do Ribeiro Frio you can find little gardens around many of the 25 forester's houses. Rare endemic and exotic plants are to be contemplated in these gardens. Especially beautiful are the forest gardens of Lamaceiros and Ribeira das Cales.

BOTANICAL GARDEN OF FUNCHAL - JARDIM BOTÂNICO

The Botanical Garden is located at the eastern border of Funchal at an altitude of about 300 m (330 yd.) and provides an outstanding overview of the subtropical flora. Both indigenous and imported plants are represented in large numbers. In 1960, the private park that had been laid out in the 19th century by the Scotch hotelier William Reid became the Jardim Botânico. Today, the former manor house (close to the entrance) accommodates the little Museu de História Natural (Museum of Natural History). A gift shop sells tasteful T-shirts, culinary souvenirs and CDs with folklore music.

The venerable park with its wells, grottos, aviaries and lookout balconies has been preserved and replenished with numerous subtropical flowers. Special sections that are dedicated for example to the coastal vegetation of Madeira or to the useful plants that are cultivated on the island have been constructed on terraces in the lower areas. Moreover you can find collections of succulents (water saving plants) and palm species from all over the world. You will also encounter interesting examples of the current Madeiran art of either piecing together ornaments of plants or of cutting out bizarre shapes. From the lower entrance you reach the adjoining Jardim dos Loiros (parrot park).

OPENING HOURS: garden: daily from 9am-18pm, closed on December, 25th; museum: Mon-Sat 9am-12.30pm and 14am-17.30pm; admission: 3 euros.
ARRIVAL BY CAR: Via Rápida (Cota 200) to interchange 13 (Camacha, Portela), then direction Funchal; car park at the lower entrance.
ARRIVAL BY BUS: urban bus lines 29,30,31 from Avenida do Mar (close to the market hall); busses run frequently.

PALHEIRO GARDENS

The park is also known as Blandy's Garden and situated between Funchal and Camacha at an altitude of about 600 m (655 yd.). The relatively chilly climate is perfectly suitable for a unique collection of subtropical plants. Especially plants from South Africa, Australia and New Zealand are plentifully represented. The area that currently sets up the Palheiro Gardens was founded about 200 years ago by the Earl Carvalhal as a preserve. He engaged a French landscape architect to design the "sunken garden" and the "lady's garden". Both are symmetrically organized gardens with flower borders, water stretches and stone sculptures. Together with a baroque chapel they are the heart of the park. In 1885, the English wine merchant family Blandy acquired the estate and developed it in the English landscape style that tries to imitate nature. This concept is most impressively realized in the Ribeira do Inferno (Inferno). A camellia avenue leads towards the colonial villa of the Blandy's family. Protea shrubs surround it. The villa is still inhabited by the family and can thus only be contemplated from the outside. Giant araucaria conifers line a brook that runs lovely trough the park. A stylish teahouse with wicker furniture from Camacha in the lower part of the park invites the visitor to have a break or to buy cut flowers and culinary souvenirs.

OPENING HOURS: Mon-Fri 9am-16pm, closed on: January, 1st; Good Friday; May, 1st; December, 25th/26th; admission: 8 euros.

ARRIVAL BY CAR: ER 102 Funchal-Camacha; pay attention to signposts; car park at the entrance; taxis are allowed to enter the park (to the villa).

ARRIVAL BY BUS: urban bus lines 36,37 from Avenida do Mar; approx. every half hour, about 20min journey.

JARDIM TROPICAL MONTE PALACE

The garden is situated at an altitude of about 500 m (547 yd.) below the church of Monte. It goes back to the park of the hotel Monte Palace that was run there from 1904 to 1965. The dense stock of indigenous laurel trees, Wax Myrtles and Madeira Junipers in combination with European and North American oak species dates back to this time. You can find Natal Lilies, azaleas and an extensive collection of tree ferns (cf. p. 11) that have been gathered by today's owner, José Berardo. A humid ravine has been laid out as an oriental garden with Buddha statues, pagodas and watercourses. The oriental garden is continued by a playful terrace garden below the former hotel. Japanese koi swim in ponds and you can also see swans. Today, the building is the seat of the Berardo Foundation that is dedicated e.g. to environmental protection. Some gnarled, about 2000 years old olive trees were saved from being flooded by a water reservoir in Portugal. At the very east of the garden you can find a section that is devoted to the endemic flora. Berardo did not only collect plants but bizarre things of all kinds. Painted tiles (Azulejos) and stonemasons' products are arranged in the garden. A museum holds giant minerals and wooden African sculptures. A glass of Madeira wine (included in the entrance) is served in the cafeteria.

OPENING HOURS: daily from 09.00am-18.00am; on Sundays only the northern entrances at the funicular station are open; admission: 10 euros.
ARRIVAL BY CAR: only a few lay-bys at the western entrance (Caminho do Monte)
ARRIVAL BY BUS: urban bus lines 20,21 from Avenida do Mar/Rua 31 de Janeiro.
ARRIVAL BY FUNICULAR: from Funchal – old town centre, daily from 10.00am to18.00pm, 15min journey.

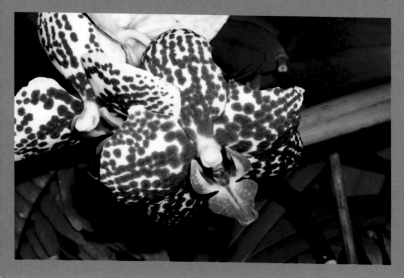

JARDIM ORQUÍDEA AND QUINTA DA BOA VISTA

The **JARDIM ORQUÍDEA** (Orchid Garden) is situated below the Jardim Botânico. An enormous variety of orchid species from all over the world has been arranged here on a very confined space the most natural way possible. According to their heritage the plants grow in green houses with different temperatures in the inside. The Austrian Josef Pregetter runs the garden. He does not only exhibit orchids but cultivates them and exports young plants that do not flower yet. Visitors can observe how the laboratory cultivation is realized. Information boards help to understand the process.

OPENING HOURS: daily from 09.00am to 18.00pm; admission: 4,90 euros.
ARRIVAL BY CAR: signposted from the access road to the Jardim Botânico.
ARRIVAL BY BUS: a 10min footpath is signposted from the lower entrance of the Jardim Botânico.

The **QUINTA DA BOA VISTA** is another popular orchid garden. The Englishwoman Betty Garton is in charge of this large estate in the eastern part of Funchal. She has dedicated herself to the cultivation of orchids for more than 30 years and won numerous prices on exhibitions. She puts the main emphasis on cultivating cymbidium plants (cf. p.51) as cut flowers but you can also contemplate other orchid species, bromelias and other exotic plants.

OPENING HOURS: Mon-Sat from 09.00am to 18.00pm; closed on holidays; admission: 2,50 euros.
ARRIVAL BY CAR: in Funchal over the Estrada Conde Carvalhal, from there on the way is signposted; only restricted parking facilities.
ARRIVAL BY BUS: urban bus line 32 from Avenida do Mar, direction Rochinha; busses run very frequently.

QUINTA JARDINS DO IMPERADOR

The estate has been accessible since 2004. The Emperor Charles of Austria spent the last weeks of his life here after the victorious powers of the 1st World War had banished him to Madeira in 1921. The 34 years old died in 1922. Works to restore the residential building are still ongoing but the "imperial gardens" already aglow again. The Englishmen David Webster Gordon founded the park at the beginning of the 19th century. The stock of trees in the upper part of the garden goes back to his days. You will find a remarkable, impressing collection of exotic, often very tall conifers from different continents. They are combined with giant deciduous trees from North America and indigenous species of the laurel forest. In spring, a carpet of agapanthus plants covers the ground below these trees. Their blooms glow in blue and white. An artificial brook feeds a pond with water lilies. Another popular attraction is the Jardim Malakof in the lower part of the garden. It was laid out in the French style in the middle of the 19th century. 66 flower borders are organized symmetrically around a well with a marble statue. A garden café is situated next to a small lookout tower. You can relax in typical wicker chairs while your view crosses two impressing Dragon Tree specimens and wanders over the bay of Funchal.

OPENING HOURS: Mon-Sat from 9.30am to 17.30pm; admission: 6 euros.

ARRIVAL BY CAR: ER 103 (Estrada dos Marmeleiros) to Monte; pay attention to the signposting about 500 m (547 yd.) below the centre (Largo da Fonte with church); only restricted parking facilities along the road.

ARRIVAL BY BUS: urban bus lines 20, 21 from Avenida do Mar/Rua 31 de Janeiro; busses run every half hour, 30min journey.

QUINTA PALMEIRA

The extensive park is situated on a mountain ridge in the upper municipal area of Funchal and belongs to a manor house of the 17th century. It is still in private ownership today. A team of gardeners is constantly working in the well-tended garden. The garden is located at an altitude of 250 m (273 yd.) and thus accommodates both tropical and subtropical plants. There are also to be seen many representatives of the indigenous flora that can only rarely be contemplated at other sites. The current garden estate goes back to the 1920ies when the Jardim das Rosas (Rose Garden) and the Jardim das Lagoas (Water Garden) with its romantic ponds were laid out. A grotto was lovingly decorated with tile fragments and snail shells. The colourful Azulejos (tile pictures) that decorate the Camões well (behind the not accessible main building) were imported from Lisbon and refer to the Portuguese discovery journeys. The greatest attraction is the so-called Columbus-window at the verge of the Rose Garden. The stone window frame has manueline ornaments in the form of grotesque faces and leaves of Acanthus (an old symbol of fertility). It once decorated the meanwhile torn down Casa de João Esmeraldo in Funchal. It is said that Columbus stayed there on his third voyage to America in 1498. One has an especially spectacular view from the niches in the window.

OPENING HOURS: Mon-Fri, 09pm-12pm and 14am-17am; admission: 5 euros.
ARRIVAL BY CAR: from Funchal (centre) through the Rua 31 de Janeiro and the Rua da Torrinha, direction Monte; then follow the signposting through the Rua da Levada de Santa Luzia; it is permitted to drive up to the garden.
ARRIVAL BY BUS: urban bus lines 25, 26 from Avenida do Mar.

QUINTA DO SANTO DA SERRA

The wine merchant family Blandy constructed its first country estate at the beginning of the 19th century and created an extensive park. Today the public authorities own it. The park is located at an altitude of 600 m (655 yd.) and the chilly, humid climate is perfect for plants of the Asian monsoon regions. Rhododendrons, azaleas and camellias thrive especially well here. A hydrangea avenue leads to the both wild and romantic flower garden with its giant trees, rhododendron hedges and gravel and pavement paths. It surrounds the manor house, typically painted in old rose. It is not accessible for visitors. The former stables accommodate a little zoo with fallow dear, kangaroos and ponies. The adjoining picnic space with tables and benches is valued as a popular destination for weekend excursions by the Madeirans. Behind the manor house the park moves on to orchads,

later to a eucalyptus forest. But there are also many other interesting tree species to be discovered in the gardens. At the lower verge the lookout balcony Miradouro dos Ingleses offers a spectacular view over the valley of Machico up to the eastern tip of Madeira. On days with good visibility you can even see the island Porto Santo.

OPENING HOURS: daily during the day, free entrance.

ARRIVAL BY CAR: ER 207 to Santo da Serra; entrance to the park close to the central church square at the town's exit with direction to Machico; parking facilities along the road.

ARRIVAL BY BUS: line 77 (grey-yellow-white busses of the CCSG, from Funchal over Camacha), 4-7 times a day, duration: 1 hour; lines 20, 78 (green-white-cream busses of the SAM, Funchal over Machico) 2-7 times a day, duration: 1.45 hour.

PARQUE FLORESTAL DO RIBEIRO FRIO

The forest park of Ribeiro Frio offers a good overview over the flora of the laurel forest. It is located at an altitude of 800 m (875 yd.), i.e. in the lower area of the trade wind fogs zone that is especially well developed in the northeast of the island. The laurel forest was revealed in the Parque Florestal through a teaching path. The most important trees of this vegetation form are labelled with signs that indicate the Portuguese and botanic denominations. Among others you will encounter Stink Laurels, Azorean Laurels, Madeira Mahoganies and Madeira Junipers. Endemic shrubs like Melliferous Spurge and Canary Holy grow on the verge of the ground close to introduced tree ferns, camellias and rhododendrons that thrive excellently in this climate. Opposite to the park you will find the idyllic terrain of the state-owned trout farm that is also freely accessible. Young trout are raised here. Later they are given to private keepers or released in fishing ponds. The Ribeiro Frio, one of the Madeiran brooks that are most abundant in water, supplies the farm with water. Numerous endemic flowering plants of the laurel forest are to be contemplated in the garden of the trout farm. The main bloom time is in May.

OPENING HOURS: always open, free entrance.

ARRIVAL BY CAR: ER 103 Funchal-Faial up to the forester's house at the trout farm, south to the village of Ribeiro Frio; entrance to the park opposite to the forester's house; several lay-bys at the entrance, more parking facilities further up along the road.

ARRIVAL BY BUS: lines 56, 103, 138 (grey-yellow-white busses of CCSG) from Funchal, 3-4 times per day, duration: 45 min. (check route before departure, not all busses pass Ribeiro Frio).

CITY GARDENS IN FUNCHAL

The **JARDIM MUNICIPAL** (Municipal Garden) was founded in 1880. It is located centrally at the Avenida Arriaga and presents an extraordinarily sumptuous, diverse flora. Tall jacarandas and kapok trees afford shade; visitors can stop for a rest on benches or in the garden café. Other eye-catching components are White Birds of Paradise, Frangipanis and some Sausage Trees. The **PARQUE SANTA CATARINA** extends west of the city centre. It was laid out 50 years ago. Flower borders, Camphor Trees, Tulip Trees and Coral Trees line lawns and a large pond. A chapel is situated on a lookout terrace at the verge of the park. It is dedicated to Saint Catherine and gave the park its name. You will find another idyllic garden café in the Parque Santa Catarina. The **QUINTA VIGIA** adjoins directly to the park. In the 19th century the manor house accommodated illustrious guests like the empress of Brazil. Today it is the office of the Madeiran president. Various tropical trees and shrubs densely populate a part of this beautiful garden. Entwined paths cross the flowerbeds in the rear part that faces the harbour. Many plants are labelled with their botanical denominations in these three gardens.

OPENING HOURS: Jardim Municipal and Parque Santa Catarina: always open; Quinta Vigia: mostly accessible Mon-Fri during office hours; free entrance to all of them.

ARRIVAL BY CAR: lay-bys along the Avenida do Mar, car park at the casino (Avenida do Infante), multi-storey car parks in the Rua Gulbenkian and Rua São Francisco; all of them are subject to a charge.

ARRIVAL BY BUS: numerous lines from all parts of the islands, moreover urban busses; stop: Avenida do Mar.

QUINTA DAS CRUZES AND QUINTA MAGNÓLIA

The **QUINTA DAS CRUZES** has a lovely garden with exotic plants. It was founded in the 18th century and includes a small archaeological park. There you can see coat of arms, crosses and memorial slabs, saved by collectors from torn down houses and churches. Two manueline windows you can see in the main garden that combines baroque and romantic elements. In the upper part you will find a little orchid stock. The former manor house accommodates a museum that exhibits furnishings of the 17th – 19th century.

OPENING HOURS: garden: daily 10am-18pm, entrance free; museum: Tue-Sat 10am-12.30pm, 14pm-17.30pm; admission: 2,50 Euros.
ARRIVAL BY CAR: car park at the Cota 40 (at the corner to Rua dos Ferreiros), from there on a 10min walk.
ARRIVAL BY BUS: urban line 15 A from Avenida do Mar; busses run every 10min.

The then American consul founded the park of the **QUINTA MAGNÓLIA** in the 19th century. At the beginning of the 20th century the plant collection was enriched with palm species from all over the world by the then owner, the British Dr. Herbert Watney. Later the estate belonged to the British Country Club and a sports complex was added (swimming-pool, tennis courts, etc). Today the Quinta Magnólia is owned by the public authorities and all the facilities are freely accessible (enrolment is partly required).

OPENING HOURS: daily 9am-19pm, free entrance.
ARRIVAL BY CAR: restricted parking facilities behind the entry; others along the Rua da Casa Branca or around the stadium Barreiros..
ARRIVAL BY BUS: urban lines 5, 6, 8 and 45 from Avenida do Mar; busses run frequently.

Register

REGISTER

REGISTER

Register

REGISTER

Layout: Günther Roeder, Oliver Breda
Photographs: Susanne Lipps, Oliver Breda
Production: Druckhaus Cramer, Greven
Translation: Daniela Overkamp

© Oliver Breda Verlag, Duisburg
E-mail: webmaster@bredaverlag.de
1. Edition 2006

ISBN 3-938282-09-6

TRAVEL NOTES